ACTIVE LEARNING

Games to Enhance Academic Abilities

BRYANT J. CRATTY

University of California, Los Angeles

PRENTICE-HALL, INC., Englewood Cliffs, New Jersey 07632

Library of Congress Cataloging in Publication Data

CRATTY, BRYANT J.
    Active learning.

    Includes bibliographies.
    1. Educational games.   I. Title.
LB1029.G3C7   1985   371.3'07'8   84-22323
ISBN 0-13-003468-1
ISBN 0-13-003443-6 (pbk.)

Editorial/production supervision and
    interior design: Patricia V. Amoroso
Cover design: Debra Watson
Manufacturing buyer: Harry P. Baisley

Printed in the United States of America

10 9 8 7 6 5 4 3 2 1

ISBN 0-13-003468-1   01
ISBN 0-13-003443-6 {pbk.}   01

PRENTICE-HALL INTERNATIONAL, INC., *London*
PRENTICE-HALL OF AUSTRALIA PTY. LIMITED, *Sydney*
EDITORA PRENTICE-HALL DO BRASIL, LTDA., *Rio de Janeiro*
PRENTICE-HALL CANADA INC., *Toronto*
PRENTICE-HALL HISPANOAMERICANA, S.A., *Mexico City*
PRENTICE-HALL OF INDIA PRIVATE LIMITED, *New Delhi*
PRENTICE-HALL OF JAPAN, INC.,*Tokyo*
PRENTICE-HALL OF SOUTHEAST ASIA PTE. LTD., *Singapore*
WHITEHALL BOOKS LIMITED, *Wellington, New Zealand*

Contents

Games

CHAPTER 6   *Letters, Spelling, and Reading*   92

CHAPTER 7   *Communication: Talking and Writing*   125

Preface to the Second Edition

This edition integrates new techniques and strategies into the material presented in the previous edition. The new materials expand on methodologies that have emerged in the 1970s and early 1980s. The first edition of this book reflected work conducted in the 1960s and 1970s in over thirty elementary schools in central Los Angeles. This work was based in the belief that an "active approach" to traditional academic tasks would be useful and viable. Our research at the time and research done since—both our own and that of others—reinforces this belief.

The earlier edition attracted a great deal of attention, judging from the appearance of similar works, and from the translation of that edition into several foreign languages, including German, Dutch, Spanish, and Portugese. It was even transcribed into Japanese characters, so that children in that country could better learn English!

Moreover, the first edition provided some of the impetus for my involvement in workshops, courses, and research programs in most of the states in our Union, as well as in over twenty foreign countries. I was invited to these gatherings in the capacity of "visiting expert." But, in truth, this exposure to others who dared to be innovative by using action to teach taught *me* a great deal about using movement in learning and exposed me as well to some of the limitations of the methodology. Thus I was not only a visiting lecturer; I was also a spy!

This new edition reflects the influence of two useful educational models. The first of these was initially introduced by Muska Mosston, as part of the "spectrum of teaching styles" he began developing in the 1960s. The second model is more recent. It involves the pairing of what was previously called "cognitive theory" with traditional behavioral modification. This exciting wedding of thought and behavior modification methods, termed *cognitive-behav-*

ioral modification or *cognitive-behavioral therapy*, is based on the premise that in order to change behavior—to learn new habits, responses, and ways of thinking—one must modify the thoughts that underlie that behavior. Most of the time these attempts to change habits and ways of behaving through adjusting thoughts have involved aiding the learner to engage in meaningful *self-talk*. This methodology is found within several sections of this new edition.

This book, like its predecessor, does not attempt to provide ways for physical educators to somehow "class up their acts" by providing a curriculum that closely matches that of the classroom teacher. If the physical educator is not convinced, and cannot convince others, that his or her program contains an abundance of useful material intended to improve skill, fitness, and basic motor qualities, he or she has missed the point. The thrust of this edition, as was true of the first edition, is to provide ways in which parents, curriculum specialists, child development experts, as well as teachers of normal and atypical young-sters, may use action as a helpful learning tool.

The present edition has been substantially reorganized. For example, chapters dealing with number identification and letter recognition are now combined with material that naturally proceeds from these qualities, such as mathematics and reading. In addition, three new chapters have been included. One involves materials that pair language and speech instruction with physical activity. A second contains games for gifted and creative children (who according to some estimates comprise about 90 percent of the population of children in our schools!). The final chapter of the first edition, which focused upon the awkward child, has been replaced by a chapter that outlines provocative ways in which an active curriculum may be expanded to include opportunities for a child to engage in an increasing number of decisions within the educational process. This same section of the text suggests ways in which the teacher may encourage the learner to explore new ways of thinking as well as ways in which both teacher and learner may sample and come to understand some of the components of intelligence that have been uncovered by various cognitive theorists.

I owe debts to many who assisted me in the research undergirding this book. Sister Margaret Mary Martin helped me to organize and carry out our initial investigations in this area almost twenty years ago. Her successor, Sister Mark Szczpanik, helped to further this work in the early 1970s. To both of them I give my thanks. More recently the principal, Mrs. Hawkins, and the staff of the Warner Ave. School near UCLA have helped me and my staff by affording us the use of children as subjects and as clients, upon whom we could try the various techniques and strategies emerging from our work. Finally, numerous graduate and undergraduate students have conducted special studies, exploring the ways in which action pairs in useful ways with thought, as well as how human intelligence itself seeks to work in an action environment. I am grateful for their energy, inspiration, and help.

BRYANT J. CRATTY

CHAPTER 1

Introduction

This book is about physical activity, but it is not about physical education or athletics. It is about how children can learn, but not about classroom teaching techniques. It indicates how learning can be made a happy experience by including in the process various games and physical activities. It illustrates fun-filled techniques for teaching basic academic operations that have formerly been pounded into children's psyches in less than happy ways.

This approach is not entirely new; neither does it represent some kind of educational cure-all. Educators, parents, and teachers are constantly deluged with learning panaceas. Educational overkill in the form of expansive and unsupported claims for new educational practices may be as destructive to the curriculum as certain kinds of military overkill techniques may be to mankind. The new ways of teaching described in this book will not replace other, more traditional methods, but should make learning more palatable and effective.

The general approach outlined here was originally spawned several centuries ago. Educators in France and Germany in the late 1700s and early 1800s observed that children are active beings who become joyful when they are permitted to move freely. These educators believed that children *need* movement: if the need is stifled, children will likely perform less capably in a variety of traditional learning tasks. As a result of these insights, unstructured and structured play experiences were introduced into some schools (Cratty 1972).

These educational philosophers of two and three centuries ago viewed activity much as do many current educators. They seemed to say, when constructing their programs, that movement should be introduced in the schools for two main reasons: (1) to produce more relaxed and joyful children, who would be willing learners within the classroom, and (2) to release children's tensions that might inhibit their efforts to learn. In this text, bodily movement is viewed not as a way to reduce unpleasant overtones of classroom learning but as a method to be incorporated directly into the learning of academic operations usually taught in a restrictive environment.

The games found in this text also reflect modern theory and practices in education. The ideas of contemporary researchers who have advocated that freedoms be gradually extended to the learner (see especially the works of Muska Mosston [1966, 1982]) have been combined with recent models of the nature of developing intellectual competencies in children and youth.

Foremost among these models is that of *cognitive-behavior modification* (also called *cognitive-behavior therapy*), which began to be developed in the 1970s. This model joins a relatively straight-forward stimulus-response explanation of learning with ideas advanced by "cognitive" psychologists. Advocates of this emerging model, including Donald Meichenbaum (1977) and others, postulated that in order to modify behavior one must try to change the thoughts that underlie what people do. Using procedures that often involved adjusting the ways in which individuals engage in internal speech (or *self-talk*), clinicans have been successfully aiding people to overcome negative mental-emotional states including depression, aggression, and anxiety (Kendall and Finch 1979). Superior athletes have also been exposed to these methods in efforts to improve their skills and to help them overcome fears connected with performance (Cratty 1984). A discussion of ways in which these procedures may exert a positive influence upon a child's attention span, self-control, and learning strategies is included in the presentation of many of the activities in this book.

Other models reflected in this text build on new understandings of how children and youth develop the ability to think clearly and efficiently. Recent research has revealed that as a child matures, she begins to spend more time thinking about thinking (Flavell 1979). Contemporary theoreticians have advocated strategies that encourage this kind of "meta-cognitive" activity; they have suggested that children should not only be encouraged to think but should also be taught how to analyze and improve their thoughts and thought processes—to think about their thinking. The five year old finds it difficult to remember a lot of things at one time, but an older child attacks the memorization of a list of items in a relatively organized way. The development of such an organized method involves a specific and self-conscious effort. In the course of making such effort the child learns how to learn. Awareness of this process of thinking-about-thinking is woven into many of the activities contained in this second edition.

My recent work (Cratty 1980, 1981) and that of some researchers in Europe (Picq and Vayer 1968) has also resulted in the development of some less theory-laden methods. These methods use movement experiences to aid children to break the difficult codes that confront them when learning to read and write a language and to use mathematical symbols. Children perceive letters and numerals as nonsense shapes initially, and the rules for their combination and manipulation are at first mysterious and confusing. The coding games contained in this book offer powerful and exciting ways to help children through these difficult processes of code breaking—of giving meaning to letters, word-shapes, and numbers. Moreover, coding games, when elaborated upon, can offer an unending number of challenges to the highly creative and gifted youth in middle and late childhood as well as in adolescence (Cratty 1981).

ACTIVITY IN CLASS

Anyone who has watched children knows that they like to move. But in many classrooms relatively little movement is tolerated. Children who pay attention, sit still, cooperate, and generally maintain immobile postures during the time they are actually involved in the learning processes are the ones who get their teachers' approval.

Research data collected over the last forty years indicate that immobility may not ensure optimum intellectual learning. Since the 1960s, researchers in many parts of the world have studied how various kinds of physical activity and exercise interact with academic performance, learning, memorization, and overall school achievement. Some studies focus on academic functioning that occurs simultaneously with physical exercise, while others look at the later effects of exercise and physical activity upon learning and academic performance. The intensity of exercise, as well as the fitness levels of the subjects, has been varied. Studies have been done on the influence of action upon later memory. For example, Gutin and DiGennard (1968) found that moderate exercise facilitated improvement in addition, while, as might be expected, exhaustive exercise elicited negative learning effects immediately following this kind of work-stress.

A number of Japanese researchers have also been interested in activity-learning relationships. Matsuda and his colleagues (Matsuda and Sugihara 1969) found that after light exercise on a bicycle ergometer, subsequent learning improved in a task requiring fine discrimination. Kashiwabara and his coworkers (Kashiwabara, Kobayashi, and Kondo 1966) as well as Hayashi and his staff (Hayashi and Yamaoka 1965) found that there was a curvilinear relationship between exercise and later competence in addition tasks. Moderate exercise helped mathematical operations the most.

In two studies in the 1960s, Railo studied academic abilities and fitness relationships (Railo 1969; Railo and Eggen 1967). He found that in some cases it was stressful for relatively fit students to be subjected for long periods of time to the immobility traditionally seen in most classrooms. Children with high fitness levels, and thus hypothetically high need to move, posted successively lower grades in both academic tasks and intelligence tests when confined too long to a testing situation. This data seems to confirm the hypthesis that many children learn best when movement is a part of their learning regime. Further substantiating this assumption is data obtained by Kronby (1968), reflecting the fact that children exercising on a treadmill to 45 percent of their maximum ability performed better in mathematics tasks engaged in at the same time the exercise was taking place.

Highly pertinent to the focus of this text are contemporary investigations in which movement has been paired with tasks requiring later retention. For example, Saltz and Donnerwerth-Nolan (1981) found that movement facilitated the memorization of sentences containing various "action themes" when the children were permitted to act out the themes as the sentences were read. Levin (1976) also found that the memorization of objects was facilitated if, during the practice, the subjects/children were permitted to handle the objects (toys) presented to them.

Additionally, it has been found that relieving the pressure of too many school hours by intervals of physical education and recreation often leads to better educational and intellectual performance. In several studies, made in a variety of cultural circumstances, it has been found that (a) there seems to be an optimal number of hours during which children may be confined physically to classrooms, after which less than effective learning takes place; and (b) reduction of the hours in this kind of "pressure-setting" usually results in increased learning. It is false to assume that, if children attain high levels of learning within a five-to-six-hour school day, simply increasing the number of hours per day will result in even greater school success (Oliver 1958; Matsuda 1969). Educators who make this assumption usually discover rather quickly the law of diminishing returns. Twelve hours per day at school will not double the learning of children who formerly worked for only six hours. Indeed, the opposite effect is usually encountered. Children who study more than five or six hours per day learn less than children who work within the five-to-six-hour range. Studies of normal school children in a suburb of Paris and of developmentally delayed English children (Cratty 1973) have supported these findings and have indicated that relief of pressure during the normal five-to-six-hour day in the form of rests and of recreational and physical educational activities will tend to accelerate learning rather than diminish academic learning and classroom achievements.

Researchers have concluded that there are children of various learning types. Some learn best by passively taking in what is presented to them by their teachers; others learn best by doing and being physically active when they learn. Furthermore, it seems that healthy children with high activity needs become increasingly inhibited in the effort they bring to intellectual efforts the longer they are confined to a classroom. These active children are not dumb and do not become dumb when sitting; they just become unable to apply appropriate effort in passive situations when their personalities and needs literally cry for movement (Railo 1967, 1968; Matsuda and Sugihara 1968; Ryan 1969).

TOO MUCH ACTIVITY

Particularly within recent years, certain groups of children have attracted the attention of physicians, psychologists, and educators. These are the children who are *too active* most of the time at home, in classrooms, or wherever they happen to alight momentarily. These children are said to be hyperactive. They move too much and in inappropriate ways; they leave their seats too often to please the teacher; when they are in their seats, they often keep their eyes and hands busy in tasks not related to what is happening in the classroom.

Several approaches have been used on these children, and some of them have been helpful. Often the children are placed on medication that tends to slow down their activity but does not dull them intellectually. At times the children are placed in (or may choose to go into) small office-like cubicles where they can concentrate on their schoolwork without distraction. Relaxation exercises and practice in slow motions have also helped to curb hyperactivity.

Probably some of these active children (usually boys) were not always much more active than many of their fellow students. However, their active behavior may have been punished inordinately by teachers or may have attracted the censure of parents and other authority figures. This adult punishment, instead of calming them down, had the reverse effect. Some became mildly emotionally disturbed, and this disturbance was reflected in increased levels of activity. Hyperactivity may also be a way for some children to block out disturbing demands made on them by adults who seek to control them excessively.

Although it is certainly necessary to help such children to calm down, at the same time it seems possible to adjust the school curriculum in part so that it matches more closely some of the movement needs of some of the children participating.

Contemporary research in Sweden (Setterlind 1983) and studies I am currently assisting with in Italy involving relaxation training of school children reflect current interest in the manner in which a child may be encouraged to relax in order to learn better. Other contemporary studies are focusing upon a large group of relatively normal children, and an attempt has been made to help them adjust their levels of activity to those that are optimum and to seek pleasure by learning to relax. Investigations, including the ones in which I am engaged, first attempt to identify children and youth whose attention spans are diminished, and then to involve them in periodic sessions of calming and relaxing activities to improve their levels of attention and classroom self-control (Cratty and Savelli 1984).

In one of the newer trends found in methodological and scientific literature, attempts are being made to incorporate *self-talk* into movement tasks, reflecting appropriate planning strategies as well as good methods to use when doing a task, and effective cognitive strategies to employ after a task is completed. While performing a motor task, the child is encouraged to say things to himself or herself that reflect good cognitive management skills. After slowing the child down by using these self-talk techniques during motor tasks, it is hoped that the child will then begin to think more about the planning and execution of classroom tasks, thereby facilitating their execution. In general, it has been found that this kind of transfer of cognitive strategies from motor to academic tasks will be successful if the parallels between the two tasks, and the reasons for the self-talk, are carefully explained to and understood by the child (Cameron and Robinson 1980). Some of the games contained in Chapter 2, Calming Down and Tuning Up, reflect this kind of technique to calm and focus children evidencing hyperactivity.

INDIVIDUAL DIFFERENCES

The intelligence testing movement in this century was in part stimulated by the need to evaluate men for military service in World Wars I and II. The military research led to more general testing endeavors. Parents and teachers became interested in identifying highly intelligent or gifted children. The word *gifted* has largely gone out of style over the past two decades and has been replaced by the labels *creative* and *talented*. The use of these new words has signalled the emergence of a more healthy concern for recognizing the various abilities of children. It has been suggested that from 90 to 100 percent of all children are probably talented in at least one area. But standardized intelligence tests do not always reflect the individual talents of each child. Creative children—children who are able to produce new insights about their world—do not always pass I.Q. tests with flying colors.

Despite the continued proliferation of interest in these creative and talented children, relatively little has been done to pique their interest in physical activity. Though studies have indicated that increased physical activity will do much to assist the development of the talents of creative children who do not respond well to the traditional classroom environment, little has been done to design special motor development programs for them (Torrance 1971). Chapter 8 was written to fill this gap. It is hoped that the activities in this section will challenge creative and talented children by capturing their interest and engaging their intellects.

The use of vigorous action as a teaching tool has historically played an important role in the education of less able children, youth, and adults. One of the first uses of motor activity in education was described in the writings of French educators of the deaf around the last part of the eighteenth century. In their efforts to educate the legendary "Wild Boy of Aveyron" Itard and Sequin employed a number of active games (Itard 1932).

Both the very young and the intellectually less capable can benefit from learning in happy, active ways. Action required as a close accompaniment to learning motivates children. Physical involvement in a thoughtful exercise, particularly when accompanied by vocalizations, together with an opportunity for close visual inspection of what is going on promotes a high level of involvement and attention on the part of learners, even those whose attention spans are poor. Additionally, performance in such exercises demonstrates immediately and obviously whether or not the concept or academic operation in question has been acquired. Teachers are thus provided with vivid and visible information by which to gauge the progress of each child. Thus both teachers and children at all points on the academic continuum may benefit from the inclusion of some active learning operations within the total school day or week.

It has finally been realized that the handicapped should not be excluded from everyday society. Their inclusion, it has been decided in the United States, should begin with experiences during the school years that permit those impaired in various ways to interact with a broad spectrum of their peers. Laws both at the Federal and local levels have expedited the integration of the so-called handicapped child and youth with his or her peers, both in academic contexts and in physical education and competitive sport programs. This trend of combining the personalities and skills of both the typical and atypical child is reflected in several of the activities offered in the following chapters.

OVERVIEW

Sophisticated school administrators, curriculum supervisors, teachers, and parents are asking themselves whether the new methods of teaching classroom skills really are more helpful than the more traditional approaches. This questioning is a healthy sign, I believe, for too often educational practices that have been less than sound have been incorporated too rapidly into the school curriculum without the necessary verification in the form of valid research findings. The concept of educational overkill was previously alluded to in this chapter.

Particular skepticism should be directed toward any technique—whether balance-beam walking, visual training, or crawling on the floor—that is vastly different from the classroom operation it is purported to remedy. Generally, the proponents of these types of extraclassroom techniques state rather emphatically that their methods will indeed "transfer" in direct ways back into the classroom and aid in resolving a variety of educational, intellectual, and perceptual problems of children.

If a technique that does not specifically involve spelling is purported to help spelling, sufficient proof of two things should be supplied before this technique is taken up: (1) that taking an indirect course to teach spelling is more helpful than teaching spelling in the direct ways now usually employed; and (2) that the unusual remedial techniques employed will truly transfer in a direct way to spelling.

More and more, unusual claims for the remedying of a variety of educational, perceptual, and/or intellectual problems using simple sensory-motor activities have been scrutinized by careful researchers. I have in several reviews, for example, examined the claims made by those espousing a "sensory-integrative" approach to the solving of educational problems and to "energizing" the higher centers (Cratty 1980, 1981). Like other models that periodically make appearances, "sensory-integrative therapy" purports to somehow train, or make more healthy, the central nervous system. Advocates of this method propose that a variety of problems can be solved by simply exposing the child to a relatively narrow range of sensory and motor activities intended to stimulate centers in the brain stem.

I cannot make this type of grandiose claim for the benefits of the games that follow. However, research extending back into the 1960s supports the educational value of movement activities that are paired in precise and intelligent ways with academic and problem-solving skills (Pharnes 1968; Cratty and Martin 1971; Cratty and Szczpanik 1970; Grabbard and Shea 1979; Van Osdol, Johnson, and Geiger 1974; Thornburg and Fisher 1970). Indeed it is remarkable how wide a variety of academic, pre-academic, and cognitive tasks have been combined with vigorous action with positive results in recent years. There is literally no component of the elementary school or secondary school curriculum that has not been made more palatable to youth through teaching techniques that permit children to both move and think at the same time. These curriculum inroads have affected the teaching of such diverse subjects as foreign languages (using a method called "total physical response") (Asher 1969) and high school physics (Johns 1971). Ideas usually found in college level courses dealing with political science, social psychology, and psychology have been translated into movement experiences for elementary and secondary school curricula (Cratty 1975). Traditionally taught pre-reading and basic quantitative skills become more vivid learning experiences when wedded to movement (Grabbard and Shea 1979; Ross 1970; Humphrey 1966; Hendrickson and Muehl 1962).

Among other interesting trends in educational methods is the conceptual approach to reducing hyperactivity and prolonging attention suggested by Palkes and Kahona (1968) and developed further in studies by Strommer (1973); Glenwick and Burka (1975); and Meichenbaum and Goodman (1969). (These studies are summarized in Kendall and Finch [1979].) Interesting related studies include Palkes, Stewart, and Freedman's (1972) work with verbal pre-training; Karoly and Kanfer's (1974) work with contracts made with the child prior to approaching tasks; and Debus's (1970) and Ridberg, Parke, and Hetherington's (1971) work with observation and discussion of well-controlled models of appropriate behavior. These useful strategies are found in the new chapters of this edition.

One recent trend in educational methods that I do *not* endorse is that which advocates that teachers "throw open the doors completely" to student participation. The microsociety represented by the teaching–learning milieu must have rules about who decides what. When no such rule structure is maintained, chaos results. It is possible to allow student participation in decision-making while still maintaining the necessary level of structure. Muska Mosston (1966, 1982) pioneered the development of programs of this sort in the 1960s. His advocacy of a gradual granting of greater and greater amounts of decisionmaking responsibility to students caught the attention of many in physical education as well as in general education. While his approach is sometimes misunderstood and at times misapplied, many have understood and have truly encouraged their students to think about the content of their own educations, and about the planning and outcomes of curricular offerings. Mancini et al. (1983) have summarized the results of studies in which this approach has been considered. Essentially, the investigations of student-centered planning and decisionmaking demonstrate clearly the positive difference in student attitudes that is created when students are permitted to participate in the planning and execution of their own programs. Many of Mosston's ideas and concepts are being evaluated by contemporary researchers interested in identifying exactly what kinds of social-emotional and/or intellectual competencies are likely to be the result of exposing children to movement curricula in which the learner is able to make various kinds of decisions (Schempp, Cheffers, and Zaichkowsky 1983). Attitude change as well as motor skill development have also been studied as possible outcomes of Mosston's approach (Mancini, Cheffers, and Zaichkowsky 1976; Martinek, Zaichkowsky, and Cheffers 1977). In general, it has been found that carefully extending useful decisions to children within the context of a movement lesson will elicit change in a variety of qualities, including their self-concept and attitudes about physical activity. The manner in which the activities in this book may be taught so that the learner participates in their modification is explained in the discussions of many of the games that follow.

In working with the games that follow, an awareness of the various types of thinking processes involved in each activity may be helpful. Cognitive psychologists began to formulate lists of human intellectual abilities in the 1960s (Gagne 1965; Guilford 1968). Among the abilities identified are

The ability to analyze problems.   To take problems apart and examine their components.

The ability to synthesize.   To combine smaller "pieces" of thought or component parts of a problem in unique ways.

Ability to evaluate.   Ability to judge oneself and others and to make increasingly finer discriminations with age, based upon increasingly subtle and sophisticated criteria.

Memory.   Thorough researchers usually divide this important human intellectual ability into several categories: short-, medium-, and long-term memory; the memory of various kinds of events and of different stimuli (auditory, visual, tactile, etc.).

Convergent production.   The ability to search for and discover the best solution to a problem (an ability often called upon in the "hard sciences").

Divergent production.   The ability to discover a variety of solutions to a single problem (an ability often called upon in movement education programs and in the performing and graphic arts).

Awareness of which of these intellectual operations is called upon in various tasks may aid you in helping students to deal with decisionmaking, and it offers you an opportunity to present problems in a variety of ways in order to involve your students in a variety of intellectual operations. The final chapter elaborates on these possibilities.

Though the work is based on the understanding that movement may facilitate learning, I do not assume that "movement is the basis of intelligence." I feel that, essentially, "intelligence is the basis of intelligence," and that thought and knowledge acquisition may be accomplished through either passive or active (that is, physically interactive) processes. (See Cratty 1979 for fuller treatment of this philosophy, described in terms of a model of human development.)

This "cognitive approach" of mine differs from the model of intelligence espoused by Piaget. Piaget believed that action was the basis of intelligence. In his autobiography, for example, he suggests that he was led to this conclusion because of his early exposure to retarded children. Since they lacked speech, and yet could apparently reason, Piaget concluded that action, not language, was the basis of cognitive growth in children (Piaget 1952).

The simplistic assertion that "movement is the basis of thought" fails, however, to explain adequately how armless and legless children can perform at intellectual levels equal to those of normal children (Decarie 1969), how an individual with cerebral palsy can obtain an advanced degree, how it is that some gifted children are measurably physically awkward, or how some children who have difficulties learning academic tasks well are able to perform physical tasks with ease. My prolonged contact with atypical children has led me to formulate a model that explains the acquisition of intelligent behaviors not only by the normal but by the less-than-able child and youth as well.

A thorough perusal of Piaget's writings might be well undertaken by those who superficially and glibly postulate that movement is an imperative base of intelligence. Their searches would uncover evidence that even when observing his normally functioning children Piaget noted a remarkable number of intellectual qualities well within the earlier stages of his "sensory-motor period." These included the child awareness of means-ends relationships, his ability to experiment with new motor and sensory experiences, and abilities that reflected the formulation of new combinations of *scheme*; all qualities found within the lists of those exploring human intelligence in thorough experimental ways (Piaget 1952a).

Indeed, excerpts from Piaget's final writings indicate that the famous Swiss scholar viewed the "action base" to learning in a more cognitive manner than many currently believe. He states, for example, that "Action ... is only constructive when it involves the participation of the child himself. . . . It is absolutely necessary that they form ... hypotheses, and verify them (or not verify them) through ... their own active manipulations" (Piaget 1973). Further clarifying what Piaget meant by *the action base to learning*, those who have worked with him have written, "Being cognitively active does not mean that the child merely manipulates. . . . He can be mentally active without physical manipulation, just as he can be mentally passive while actually manipulating objects" (Inhelder et al 1974). The content of this book uses purposeful action, action containing hypotheses, and movement combined with quality of thought.

I have offered this brief look at the theoretical background for this book in the hope that it would be helpful to those exploring the subject or in understanding the context in which my work has developed. This book is not, however, a text about theories and educational models. Essentially the manual is meant to be a practical *methods* book. Learning theorists call the approach these methods reflect *narrow transfer width*. That is, the understanding that you must closely design the content of educational programs to match precisely those goals you have set for yourself. Those who claim a rather broad transfer width for their methods are generally received with more enthusiasm than those, like myself, who claim only a narrow transfer width. It is heartening and inspiring to many to believe that the use of a few simple sensory or motor activities will transfer broadly to a wide range of academic operations and human abilities. I just do not believe that the research supports the hopes and claims of the more enthusiastic of the sensory-integrativists, sensory-motorists, and others who advocate this latter kind of optimistic viewpoint.

Many of the techniques employed do not need proof that they somehow transfer to classroom operations; indeed they *are* these same operations simply conducted in a different form. Jumping in a grid and spelling is spelling; reading a word that instructs a child to execute a movement is reading! Legitimate criticism and healthy skepticism, however, should be directed toward literal application of these techniques to large groups of intellectually capable children in middle and late childhood. This book does not represent the answer to the multitude of complex learning problems encountered by the numerous types of children presently occupying our schools. Rather it is hoped that discerning teachers, parents, and curriculum specialists will come away from this book with another helpful set of tools with which to sharpen the minds of the nation's children and youth.

THE GAMES CHILDREN PLAY

There are several other interesting relationships among fitness, games children play, and intelligence that justify the use of learning games in elementary and secondary schools. For example, one authority has recently stated that, to an increased degree, American children are choosing to play games combining the use of intelligence and strategy. This is to be expected, because the young of all civilizations generally incorporate into their games the skills they perceive as important in adulthood. The aborigine boy becomes adroit at catching small game with his father's snares, and the American girl playing doctor seems to be preparing herself for tasks she thinks she will later need for success as an adult.

If left to their own devices, American children frequently choose games requiring less and less vigorous activity, despite the fact that they have basic physical fitness needs that should be met.

With relationships between thought and physical activities in mind, some researchers have begun to incorporate more and more intellectual material into the teaching of physical skills, rather than simply demonstrating and hoping that the child will copy the movement in a mindless manner. Research has indicated that teaching children the principles of the action is often the best way to ensure acquisition of skill (Werner 1973).

Data of this nature suggest that, unless childhood games are made intellectually challenging, there may be a division created between children who play and become fit and those who withdraw from activity and exercise their intellects in passive ways (Railo 1967). Research into problems of this nature (though further research is still needed), has produced data that support the inclusion of vigorous learning games in academic programs—games combining the opportunity to gain fitness with the opportunity to learn academic skills and exercise intellectual capacities (Humphrey 1972.)

SUMMARY AND OVERVIEW

This book has been written in order to illustrate how movement activities may be combined in useful ways with tasks intended to enhance academic and intellectual abilities. The methods described in this second edition represent a healthy wedding of traditional educational models with newer models that involve explanations of cognitive development. Themes that thread through the book include operations intended to enhance memory and to improve the ways in which children and youth organize their minds when planning and executing tasks both physical and mental.

The games are intended for a variety of children, youth, and adults. Creative, gifted, and talented children are likely to be challenged by activities in several parts of the text, but the offerings in Chapter 8 are specifically designed for them. Children with learning difficulities are likewise provided with activities throughout the book, from those intended to enhance attention (Chapter 2), to those that help instill basic academic skills needed in mathematics and reading (Chapters 5 and 6).

The games and descriptions of their modifications, contain two dimensions, relative to child/learner participation. On the one hand, the instructions include discussions and ways in which the learner may begin to take an increasingly larger role in decisions that relate to the various lessons. On the other hand, tasks of increasing intellectual complexity are presented throughout the book. Various intellectual processes such as memory, evaluation, divergent and convergent thinking, as well as analysis and synthesis are called upon in many of the games. The way in which a teacher or parent may plan actitivies that extend increasing freedom to the child and at the same time provide increasingly challenging intellectual experiences is explained in the model "constructed" in the final chapter.

BIBLIOGRAPHY

ASHER, JAMES J.   The total physical response technique of learning. *Journal of Special Education*, 1969, *3*, 45-52.

CAMERON, M.I., and ROBINSON, V.M.J.   Effects of cognitive training on academic and task behavior of hyperactive children. *Journal of Abnormal Psychology*, 1980, *8*, 403-419.

CRATTY, B.J.   *Physical expressions of intelligence.* Englewood Cliffs, NJ: Prentice-Hall, 1972.

_____. *Learning about human behavior through active games.* Englewood Cliffs, NJ: Prentice-Hall, 1975.

_____. *Perceptual and motor development of infants and children.* Englewood Cliffs, NJ: Prentice-Hall, 1979.

_____. *Adapted physical education for handicapped children and youth.* Denver: Love Publishing, 1980.

_____. Sensory motor theories and practices: An overview. In R. Walk and H. Pick (Eds.), *Intersensory perception and sensory integration.* New York: Plenum, 1981a, 345-369.

_____. *Coding games.* Denver: Love Publishing, 1981b.

_____. *Psychological preparation and athletic excellence.* Ithaca, NY: Mouvement Publications, 1984.

√CRATTY, B. J., and MARTIN, SISTER M. M. *The effects of learning games upon children with learning difficulties.* Los Angeles: Dept. of Kinesiology, UCLA, Monograph, 1971.

CRATTY, B.J., and SZCZPANIK, M. *The effects of a program of learning games upon selected academic abilities in children with learning difficulties.* Los Angeles: Dept. of Kinesiology, UCLA, Unpublished Monograph, 1970.

DEBUS, R. L. Effects of brief observation of model behavior on conceptual tempo of impulsive children. *Developmental Psychology,* 1970, *2,* 22-32.

DECARIE, T. G. A study of the mental and emotional development of the thalidomide child. In B. M. Foss (Ed.), *Determinants of infant behavior.* London: Methuen, 1969, Vol. IV, 122-148.

FLAVELL, J.H. Metacognition and cognitive monitoring. *American Psychologist,* 1979, *34,* 906-911.

FLAVELL, J.H., FRIEDRICHS, A.G., and HOYT, J.D. Developmental changes in memorization processes. *Cognitive Development,* 1970, *1,* 324-340.

GAGNE, R. W. The analysis of instructional objectives for the design of instruction. In R. Glaser (Ed.), *Teaching machines and programmed learning II: Data and directions.* Dept. of Audiovisual Instruction, National Education Association, 1965, 186-203.

GLENWICK, D.S., and BURKA, A.A. Cognitive impulsivity and role taking skills in elementary school children. *Perceptual and Motor Skills,* 1975, *41,* 547-552.

√GRABBARD, C. P., and SHEA, C.H. Influence of movement activities on shape recognition and retention. *Perceptual and Motor Skills,* 1979, *48,* 116-118.

GUILFORD, J.P. *Intelligence, creativity and their educational implications.* San Diego: Knapp, 1968.

GUTIN, B., and DiGENNARO, J. Effect of one-minute and five-minute steps-ups on performance of simple addition. *Research Quarterly,* 1968 *39,* 81-85.

HAYASHI, T., and YAMAOKA, S. Research of the influence of physical activity on mental work. *Japanese Research Journal of Physical Education,* 1965, *10,* 101-107.

HENDRICKSON, L.N., and MUEHL, S. The effects of attention and motor response pre-training on learning to discriminate b, d, in kindergarten children. *Journal of Educational Psychology,* 1962, *53,* 236-241.

HUMPHREY, J. H. An exploratory study of active games in learning of number concepts by first grade boys and girls. *Perceptual and Motor Skills,* 1966, *23,* 819-822.

———. The use of motor activity learning in the development of science concepts with slow learning fifth grade children. *Journal of Research in Science Education,* 1972, *9,* 261-265.

INHELDER, B., SINCLAIR, H., and BOVET, M. *Learning and the development of cognition.* Cambridge, MA: Harvard University Press, 1974.

ITARD, J.-M.G., *The wild boy of Aveyron.* Trans. George and Muriel Humphrey. New York: Prentice-Hall (formerly Appleton-Century-Crofts), 1932.

JOHNS, R. H. Gymnasium physics. *The Physics Teacher,* 1971, *9,* 23-27.

KAROLY, P., and KANFER, F.H. Effects of prior contractual experiences on self-control in children. *Developmental Psychology,* 1974, *10,* 459-460.

KASHIWABARA, K., KOBAYASHI, T., and KONDO, M. The influence of physical activity on mental work. *Japanese Research Journal of Physical Education,* 1966, *11,* 237-239.

KENDALL, P. C., and FINCH, A. J., JR. Developing nonimpulsive behavior in children: Cognitive-behavioral strategies for self-control. In P. C. Kendall and S. D. Hollon (Eds.), *Cognitive-behavioral interventions: theory, research and procedures.* New York: Academic Press, 1979.

KRONBY, B. How a person's numerical ability is changed during different loads of physical work on the ergometric bicycle. Unpublished Report from Pedagogisk Psyckologiska Institutionen Vid. Stockholm, Sweden, 1966.

LEVIN, J.R. What have we learned about maximizing what children learn? In J. R. Levin and L. L. Allen (Eds.), *Cognitive learning in children.* New York: Academic Press, 1976.

MANCINI, V.H., CHEFFERS, J., and ZAICHKOWSKY, L. Decisionmaking in elementary school children: effects on attitudes and interaction. *Research Quarterly,* 1976, *47,* 80-85.

MANCINI, V.H., WEUST, D.A., CHEFFERS, J.T.F., and RICH, S.M. Promoting student involvement in physical education by shared decisions. *International Journal of Physical Education,* 1983, *20,* 16-23.

MARTINEK, T., ZAICHKOWSKY, L., and CHEFFERS, J. Decisionmaking in elementary age children: effects of motor skills and self-concept. *Research Quarterly,* 1977, *48,* 349-357.

MATSUDA, I., and SUGIHARA, T. An experimental research of the effect of physical activity on the mental and psychomotor function. *Japanese Journal of Physical Education,* 1969, *13,* 242-250.

MEICHENBAUM, D. *Cognitive-behavioral modifications: An integrative approach.* New York: Plenum, 1977.

MEICHENBAUM, D.H., and GOODMAN, J. Training impulsive children to talk about themselves: A means of developing self-control. *Journal of Abnormal Psychology,* 1969, *7,* 533-565.

MOSSTON, M. *Teaching physical education.* Belmont, CA: Wadsworth, 1982.

OLIVER, J.N.   The effects of physical conditioning exercises and activities on the mental characteristics of educationally sub-normal boys. *British Journal of Educational Psychology*, 1958, *28*, 155-160.

——.   The effects of physical conditioning on the sociometric status of educationally sub-normal boys. *Physical Education*, 1960, *156*, 38-46.

PALKES, S., STEWART, M., and FREEDMAN, J.   Improvement in maze performance of hyperactive boys as a function of verbal-pre-training procedures. *Journal of Special Education*, 1972, *5*, 337-342.

PALKES, S., and KAHONA, R.   Porteus maze performance of hyperactive boys after training in self-directed verbal commands. *Child Development*, 1968, *39*, 817-826.

PIAGET, J.   Forward in M. Schwebel and J. Raph (Eds.), *Piaget in the classroom.* New York: Basic Books, 1973.

——.   *The origins of intelligence in children.* New York: International Univ. Press, 1952a.

——.   Autobiography. In E. G. Boring (Ed.), *History of Psychology in Autobiography.* Worcester, MA: Clark Univ. Press, 1952b, Vol. IV, 237-256.

PICQ, L., and VAYER, P.   *Education psycho-motorice.* Paris: Editions Dion Derem et Cie, 1968.

RAILO, W.S.   Physical fitness and intellectual achievement. *Scandinavian Journal of Educational Research*, 1969, *2*, 103-120.

RAILO, W.S., and EGGEN, S.   Physical and mental endurance. Norwegian College of Physical Education and Sport, Unpublished Monograph, 1967.

RIDBERG, H. E., PARKE, R.D., and HETHERINGTON, E.M.   Modification of impulsive and reflective cognitive styles through observation of film mediated models. *Developmental Psychology*, 1971, *5*, 369-377.

ROSS, D.   Incidental learning of number concepts in small group games. *American Journal of Mental Deficiency*, 1970, *48*, 718-725.

RYAN, E.D.   Perceptual characteristics of vigorous people. In Cratty, B. J., and Brown, R. (Eds.), *New perspectives of man in action.* Englewood Cliffs, NJ: Prentice-Hall, 1969.

SALTZ, E., and DONNENWERTH-NOLAN, S.   Does motoric imagery facilitate memory for sentences? A selective interference test. *Journal of Verbal Learning and Verbal Behavior*, 1981, *20*, 323-332.

SAVELLI, M. D., CRATTY, B. J., and PISTOLETTI, A.   Relaxation training: Effects upon classroom attention and impulsivity in youth 11–14 years. Submitted to *Didatica Del Movimento* (Italy), 1984.

SCHEMPP, P.G., CHEFFERS, J.T., and ZAICHKOWSKY, L.D.   Influence of decision-making on attitudes, creativity, motor skills, and self-concept in elementary children. *Research Quarterly for Exercise and Sport*, 1983, *54*, 183-189.

SETTERLIND, S. Relaxation training in school. *Studies in Educational Sciences*, 1983, no. 43, 335.

STROMMER, E. A. Verbal self-regulation in a children's game: Impulsive errors in 'Simon says.' *Child Development*, 1973, 44, 849-853.

THORNBURG, K. R., and FISHER, V. L. Discrimination of 2-d letters by children after play with 2- or 3-dimensional letter forms. *Perceptual and Motor Skills*, 1970, *30*, 979-986.

TORRANCE, P. Psychology of gifted children and youth. In W. Cruikshank (Ed.), *Psychology of exceptional children and youth*. Englewood Cliffs, NJ: Prentice-Hall, 1971.

VAN OSDOL, R. M., JOHNSON, D.M., and GEIGER, L. The effects of total body movement on reading achievement. *Australian Journal of Mental Retardation*, 1974, *3*, 16-19.

WERNER, P. Integration of physical education skills with concepts of levers at intermediate grade levels. *Research Quarterly*, 1973, *43*, 423-428.

CHAPTER 2

Calming Down
and Tuning Up

There are some children who are habitually too excited to work effectively in classrooms. They move their bodies too much, and when apparently fixed in their seats may move their eyes about to look at everything but their school-work.

The causes for this hyperactive behavior are not always easily detectable, even by professionals. A hyperactive child may simply be immature and, like a younger child, need to physically explore the world around him to a greater degree than would be expected of a child his age. On the other hand, he may be perceptually confused; his visual apparatus may not organize the world effectively, and he may need to confirm where things are, how far away they are, and what shape objects take by actually going places and touching things. Sometimes there are slight problems in the complex mechanisms of the brain that control general bodily arousal and activity level. Or the child may have emotional problems that prevent him from concentrating for prolonged periods of time.

Children whose abilities do not match the difficulty of the school work assigned to them may also be labelled hyperactive by their teachers. A child who finds the work too easy and boring may seek to stimulate herself with activities and actions deemed inappropriate by the teacher. On the other hand, academically deficient youngsters, finding their lessons too hard, will often engage in avoidance behaviors, which the person in charge of the classroom may understand as hyperactive or intentionally disruptive. My text *Remedial Physical Activity* contains a more thorough discussion of various models intended to explain hyperactive and distractable behaviors (Cratty 1975). Indeed, motor planning of children when trying to execute complex skills may be disrupted by poor impulse control (Cratty and Gibson 1984).

Despite differences of opinion concerning just why some children are too active for their own good, there is almost unanimous opinion that an inordinate amount of activity is likely to cause learning difficulties within most educational settings. A variety of methods have been devised to aid such children to become self-controlled and better organized so that they can function well intellectually, emotionally, and socially.

In contrast to the child who moves too much and seems almost too alert is the child who seems habitually sleepy. He is lethargic, hard to interest, and difficult to alert to physical as well as intellectual tasks. He is a dreamer who seems to dream too much, at inappropriate times, and in inappropriate places. Both the active and lethargic child need to be aided to better match their levels of arousal to the tasks they find themselves confronted with in their schools.

DO CHILDREN "WEAR OUT" IN SPORTS?

Among the ways to reduce activity levels in children is to somehow drain off excess energy by requiring them, or motivating them, to engage in a great deal of physical effort. At times, this "drainage theory" does not work very well; often children who have been exposed to this approach become so "high" that they have problems sleeping the night following the vigorous activity, rather than becoming relaxed as would be expected. Physical educators, either through choice or incidentally, are responsible if children are stimulated in their games to levels too high for the classroom situation to which they usually return immediately following recess or physical education classes. High levels of activity and physiological arousal are required for games and, indeed, hyperactive children can sometimes (if their other problems are not too great) play reasonably well; however, due to defective mechanisms in the brain, they then may be unable to calm themselves down after vigorous games, unlike the normal child. They are likely to prove almost impossible to the classroom teacher after physical education classes or to their parents on returning home in the evening.

Therefore effective physical education teachers, of both average and atypical youngsters, often engage in various self-control strategies at the completion of vigorous games and sports. In this way the children are returned to classrooms in a calm state of mind and body, ready to learn and to function in effective ways in tasks that require lower levels of action than are found in exciting physical activities involving the larger muscle groups of the body.

CARRELS

Another helpful ploy often used in classrooms, and one that can be employed more widely at home, involves creating a small "office" or carrel for the child to study in. Plywood partitions placed on three sides of a small desk will cut off distracting objects and people while the child attempts to do his work. I have observed this practice used in many effective ways. For example, one teacher built two small offices of this nature at the rear of her room, and children who found themselves too overaroused to work could *choose* to go there. The fact that children in this class would frequently make this choice implies that indeed children who are too active *do not like to be this way.* Their own behavior upsets them, and, when given one or several methods to relieve their upset condition, they may eagerly take advantage of them.

MEDICATION

When children are extremely distractible it is often necessary to administer medication that may calm them and enable them and their parents and teachers to work in harmony toward common goals. Physicians (usually pediatricians or pediatric neurologists) who prescribe such drugs generally must try several types and/or dosages as each child's system reacts differently to various ones. After this testing is carried out, there should be frequent conferences among doctor, parent, and teacher as the child's behavioral changes are observed and accommodated. It is often possible to calm a child down with medications and also to slow down or remove his extraneous movements while not appreciably dulling his intellectual alertness. In a similar manner, it is often possible to improve a child's coordination and to lengthen his attention span.

A child may be kept on this type of medication for one or more years. An effort is often made to gradually reduce the dosage after six months to a year have passed. As in the use of a closed study space, children are often consciously grateful for the manner in which medication has slowed them down and enabled them to gain heightened self-control, which in turn aids them to function more effectively in a wide variety of social and academic environments. However, I have yet to encounter a physician who recommends medication who does not at the same time approve of more natural methods of aiding a child to control himself or herself.

It is frequently found that physicians work with teams of educators and psychologists in an effort to adjust and refine the child's educational program. At the same time, doctors often are aware of and approve some of the various movement strategies found in this chapter as helpful adjuncts to programs of medication for the hyperactive child.

MOVEMENT AND MUSCULAR STRATEGIES
TO ADJUST AROUSAL LEVELS

Since the 1930s numerous writings have appeared, both in the United States and abroad, outlining strategies for adjusting the activation and arousal levels of everyone from hyperactive children to over-excited athletes awaiting competition. As the decades have worn on, these ideas have been scrutinized by researchers, and the methodologies have been refined. Many of these approaches have involved some component of the muscular system, as it has been recognized that over-arousal is often accompanied by excess muscular tension or by impulses to move that are expressed in exaggerated ways (Setterlind 1983).

As early as the 1930s (Jacobson 1938) and 1940s, various ways to encourage muscular relaxation have been combined with instructions to engage in visual imagery ("imagine yourself in a quiet place"). Even more recent additions to such methods have included instructions that encourage youngsters to engage in useful controlled thought as they try to focus in on tasks more effectively (Jacobson and Lufrin 1962). Contemporary methods of this nature often include instructing a child to engage in "self talk," which is intended to change the child from one who acts upon impulse to a person who carefully and thoughtfully plans out how a problem should be solved before plunging recklessly ahead (Cameron and Robinson 1980).

The following explanations and the games that follow them offer only a brief overview of some of the potentially useful methods that may be employed to help children to calm down and to concentrate their attention upon school and recreational tasks. Accompanying this section are references to works that not only outline more operations of this kind but also provide useful models and theories that form the basis of these operations.

The placement of this chapter before chapters that contain academic material was no chance occurrence. It is believed that attention levels of good quality are important prerequisites of any kind of learning experience. Often children who are placed in so-called perceptual-motor development programs in efforts to improve their muscular coordination benefit most if much of the class time is given over to "calming down" activities of the kind found in this chapter. Their problems in "coordination" may sometimes arise from the inability to attend to physical skills rather than from the inability to execute these skill in and of themselves. The frequency of the application of these methods, however, is left to the teacher/reader. They may be given prior to as well as following excitement-producing game lessons. Often they can be usefully applied after recess. Parents sometimes appreciate greeting a relaxed child at the end of the school day, so that the conclusion of a day's schoolwork is sometimes a good time for these activities. Often the games are so satisfying to the children that they may request them at various times during the school day.

The activities that follow incorporate movement and/or adjustments of muscular tension in various ways. Many, reflecting newer trends, also include efforts to aid children to adjust the thoughts that underlie behavior. For convenience, these methods are arranged in groups, and these groups are briefly discussed in the following sections. The games themselves, however, often include a variety of approaches, some incorporating visual imagery plus muscular relaxation, some combining some type of "cognitive adjustments" with motor task performance.

RELAXATION TRAINING

The overall purpose of this type of training is to give children an awareness of the extra muscular tension they carry with them. When they become aware of this tension, it is hoped that they will then learn to control it, thus reducing hyperactivity that may accompany excess muscle tonus. Although it can be argued with some validity that muscular tension is not always accompanied by emotional upset, it is usually found that internal emotional states and outside muscular tension are more intimately connected in children than in adults. Particularly in younger boys, the association between muscle and emotion is an intimate one.

When playing these games children should be placed in comfortable positions and verbally instructed to tighten and to relax various muscle groups to varying degrees. The training might start with Game 1, in which the children try to tighten all their muscles and to alternate these contractions with periods of complete relaxation accompanied by slow, deep breathing. Following this, the training might then be continued by concentrating on various muscle groups, as indicated in Game 2.

This type of training should not be continued until the child is excessively fatigued; sessions should last at least three to four minutes and, after some practice, as long as five to ten minutes. This training should be engaged in at any time it is needed—following a family quarrel or when the child is too "high" in a classroom. More able children can often learn to administer it to themselves after a period of time with good results.

The type of instructions given to children during this training depends to a large degree on the age and sophistication of children. Older children can be given the scientific names of specific muscle groups they are attempting to tighten and relax, whereas younger children must be encouraged to the same ends by using various types of verbal imagery ("Sink deep into the mat," "Make your muscles soft as cotton").

The teacher who is perceptive and creative in the ways he or she uses imagery appropriate to the children to whom it is applied is likely to be most successful.

More and more, this type of training has been incorporated into regular school settings as well as into schools for atypical youngsters. Highly effective use of these methods is made within classes of children labelled "learning disabled," since the membership often includes distractable children. Another helpful sign has been the large number of research studies that have considered the effects of this type of training on both normal and atypical children. Their findings have included data that reflect high levels of acceptability by youngsters exposed to their use. Other findings indicate that more efficient performance of school work is not the only outcome; relaxation training also promotes the more efficient utilization of physical energy in demanding endurance tasks (Setterlind 1983).

Prolonged and Slow Movements. A second type of movement experience found in some of the games that follow involves slow and controlled movement. At times this kind of movement is embedded in tasks that require close attention. The duration of these games may be lengthened, so that increased periods of concentrated movement are required of the participants. Testing of a child's ability to move in slow and controlled ways can be a helpful diagnostic tool. Request that a child draw a line (about 30 ft. long) "as slowly as you can." Children entering school who race through this kind of assignment are likely to be those who are labelled inattentive by their teacher, according to our research. Specific training in "how-slowly-can-you-move" tasks can exert a positive effect upon other classroom operations that require self-control. Maccoby, Dowley, and Hagen (1965) have also found that this kind of task is a moderately effective predictor of scores in standard intelligence tests, tasks that also require prolonged attention.

Simple prolongation of the duration of movement tasks can be effected easily. A balance beam arrangement may be made progressively longer, while other tasks can be also lengthened in order to produce attention span demands that parallel the attention span requirements found in classrooms. Contemporary research revealed differences in this ability on the part of children with and without learning disabilities (D'Amato and Herr 1982).

We once had a boy in our program whose attention span in seconds matched his chronological age in years—9! We placed him with a student helper who encouraged him to attempt to keep a tennis ball on a 2 ft. $\times$ 2 ft. board of plywood while holding the edges of the board with either hand. His ability to engage himself in this task improved from a few seconds to several minutes. The length of time to which he was able to apply himself to classroom tasks increased in equal measure. Other research we have carried out indicates that this kind of prolongation-of-task concept (either in time, or in efforts to move more slowly) correlated well with positive changes in spelling and in letter as well as pattern recognition. Moreover, children's abilities to engage in effective motor planning, as they tried to copy movements of increased complexity, correlated positively with scores made in this type of impulsivity-control task (Cratty 1968, 1982, 1983).

To be effective, these types of tasks should incorporate the following principles:

1. They should be interesting enough and challenging enough that the child must pay relatively close attention to their execution.
2. Transfer to school tasks should be taught for. That is, the child should gain an understanding of just *why* he is playing "how slowly can you

move games" (to help you concentrate in class), instead of leaving possible transfer to chance.

3. Often "moving slowly" games may be included within relaxation-training programs, or alternated with tasks requiring vigorous and fast action. In the latter case you may determine how well the child can bring himself or herself under control again.

4. Imagery and "social models" are often used with this type of activity. For example, a poorly controlled child can be asked to be the slow-moving 'shadow' of a well-controlled child as the latter moves (Game 5). Or a child can be asked to pretend to be a marionette, while seated on the lap of an instructor, in an effort to elicit both muscular relaxation and slow, controlled movements.

Changing Thoughts to Improve Self-Control.   Children labelled hyperactive are often observed to move impulsively—without thinking—when they are confronted with challenges at school, at home, and in their neighborhoods. In the 1970s this observation led perceptive psychologists and researchers to explore what is termed *cognitive-behavioral therapy* in an effort to aid children to adopt habits reflecting careful thought as they met problems at school and in other parts of their lives. Changes that were accomplished in what children thought about as they faced problems and attempted to solve them were in turn found to lead to better self-control and improved attention span.

Cognitive-behavioral therapy combines elements of traditional stimulus-response behaviorism with more contemporary models of cognitive behavior. This general method is based upon several assumptions.

1. Thoughts, like other components of behavior, may be modified with practice.

2. Thinking underlies most behavior. Thus, to change how someone acts, one should try to modify the thoughts that control and underlie behavior.

3. One of the primary ways in which we think is through the use of subvocal, internal speech. We talk to ourselves.

4. Younger children, and older children who are judged as impulsive or hyperactive, do not instruct themselves effectively when they speak to themselves. They simply act, without giving themselves useful instructions before, during, or/and after executing a task.

5. To improve the impulsive behaviors of children and youth, one should try to improve the quality of the instructions they give to themselves. They should be aided to formulate useful, task-oriented phrases.

When carrying out this kind of intervention, the teacher or parent formulates useful task-relevant phrases, and asks the child to say these phrases aloud. Motor tasks are useful when practicing this method because physical acts may be designed so that they take up prolonged periods of time, time during which the child may utter useful "self-talk phrases." Physical tasks also permit the child to clearly observe the nature of the problem, and enable both the observer/teacher and the youngster to see clearly the results of their efforts. This high visibility of physical actions permits the child to formulate helpful self-talk phrases in subsequent efforts. Games 8 and 9 in this chapter reflect the uses of these techniques in the modification of hyperactivity.

Useful principles to follow when using this type of combination of cognitive strategy and physical performance are as follows:

1. Self-talk phrases should include sentences uttered during three different time periods, relative to task performance. These include

   (a) Preparatory, or planning phrases voiced as the task is approached. These might include, for instance, "I must think carefully about what is required in this jumping task."

   (b) Statements made while the task is being executed. These phrases can include statements reflecting both successes and problems encountered; for instance, "There, I jumped over the first rope because I was careful, but I touched the next one because I didn't pay attention!"

   (c) Phrases voiced at the completion of the task. These phrases may reflect reasons for successes and failures encountered. They may also prepare the child for another try, and may also be rewarding; for instance, "I did pretty well that time, but, if I watch my feet better, I will do better next time."

2. Self-talk phrases should be sequenced in various ways. For example, initial phrases should be very task-specific, and relate only to elements of the physical act encountered; for instance, "I should jump carefully over each rope." Later, more general kinds of self-talk statements should be required of the child; for instance, "Before I do anything I should try to find out what is required of me." These latter, more general statements may then be transferred to tasks found in the classroom.

3. Self-talk statements may also be sequenced in quanitative ways. For example, whole sentences may later be changed to sentence fragments, or even to single words. To give another example, statements first spoken aloud by the child may next be uttered more quietly while the task is being performed. Even later, the statements may be thought about subvocally in ways that are even less likely to interfere with task execution and more likely to enhance performance. Finally, when self-control and intelligent planning and execution behavior is apparent, the child may be encouraged to act without the accompaniment of even subvocal speech.

4. Research by Cameron and others (Cameron and Robinson 1980) has demonstrated that maximum transfer to classroom self-control will occur when an important principle is followed. In addition to perceptual-motor tasks, various self-management training should also be engaged in using

cognitive tasks. Although some generalization from motor task planning to classroom task planning will occur if only the former tasks are engaged in, maximum transfer will occur if self-planning and self-control self-talk is engaged in using both cognitive-academic tasks, as well as various motor tasks. Thus transfer from the motor to the mental tasks must be carefully planned.

GAME 1   Tighten and Relax

Equipment: Mats, chairs.

Method: Have children either lie down or sit in comfortable positions and then have them alternately tighten and relax their total bodies ("Tighten as hard as you can ... everything ... tighter"). The tightening phase should last from three to six seconds and be followed by instructions to relax completely or some instructions compatible with the children's levels of understanding ("Become a cloud," "Take the bones out of your muscles"). After several of these contractions the children should be asked to tighten one-half as hard as they can; after a few times, half as hard as that (one-fourth as hard as maximum). All tightening phases should be interspersed with relaxed and deep breathing ("Take a deep breath and let it out completely").

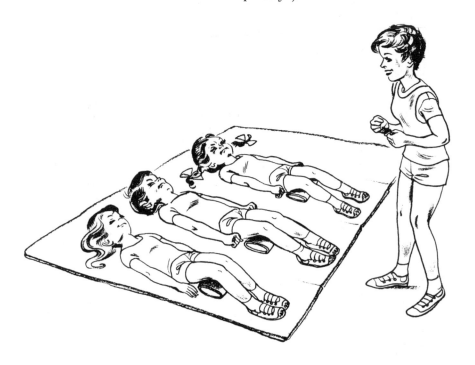

Modifications: Children can be in seated positions, heads on desks, lying on mats. Children can have padding placed under their knees to induce relaxed slight flexion at knees; pillows under head. Duration of time may vary from a few minutes to from five to ten minutes, depending on the ages and mental ability of the children. The words used can vary according to the same criterion.

GAME 2   Head to Toe and Back Again

Equipment: Mats, pads for comfort.

Method: Start with the top of the body and ask children to tighten face, then relax; then neck, shoulders, arms, hips, on down the body; alternate with periods of relaxation and deep breathing. Then up the body again: feet, hips, arms. This may be repeated several times up and down.

Modifications: Concentrate on specific muscle groups within body parts—that is, fists or upper arms. Experiment with partial contractions (one-half, one-fourth) after full contraction and reasonably complete relaxation are achieved. This technique may be used in conjunction with or after Game 1 in this series.

The teacher may lift a child's limb and, if tension is required, ask the child to hold it at a 45 degree angle to the ground, for varying periods of time. Or relaxation may be assessed if the teacher lifts a limb and then asks the child to drop it to the ground when it is released.

SLOW, CONTROLLED MOVEMENT

During the end of a session of relaxation training, it is often helpful to encourage children not simply to tighten muscles in an immobile fashion, but to move in slow, controlled ways.

GAME 3   How Slowly Can You . . . ?

Equipment: Clock, blackboard, mats, tape for making lines.

Method: One or more children can see how slowly they can move in various ways ("Draw a line as slowly as you can," "Get up from the mat as slowly as you can," "Walk a line as slowly as you can"). Clock time and give child evidence of improvement. Charts may be made showing improvement.

Modifications: More than one child can compete in one task at a time. Competition can be held in several dissimilar tasks, like line drawing, walking, getting up and down, with a child at each task.

GAME 4   Don't Drop It!

Equipment: Various materials can be used, such as a Ping-Pong ball on a spoon or a bean bag on the head.

Method: Place children on their backs, with a bean bag on their heads. See if they can get up keeping bag in place. Have slow races seeing if they can keep bags on head or a small ball on a spoon they are holding.

Modifications: Individual children can be clocked. Slow ascents and descents from mat can be alternated with faster movements. Different tasks can be done at the same time by different children with competition introduced.

GAME 5   Me and My Shadow

Equipment: Line, mats.

Method: Pair children off. Have one designated as the slow mover and the other as "his shadow." The shadow tries to match exactly the movements of

the other child. Movements must be made slowly to be copied. Experiment with a variety of movements.

Modifications: Observer can say whether "shadow" is really copying correctly; if not, then observer and shadow change roles. Limb movements, hand-finger movements, and total body movements can be employed together or in various combinations.

It is not always appropriate to teach children simply to move slowly like zombies as would result if only games similar to Games 3 through 5 were employed. As can be seen in Game 6, it may prove helpful, after finding that children can truly control their movements and move slowly, to vary the speed with which they move—to see whether they can be excited, aroused, and then bring themselves "down" again.

GAME 6 Fast and Slow

Equipment: Blackboard, mats, lines.

Method: After children develop a minimum of self-control, see if they can vary force and speed and then return to controlled movement ("How slowly can you get up? Now how fast can you get down?" "Run as fast as you can from here to there and then move as slowly as possible").

Modifications: Both fast and slow races can be introduced. The child can be asked to alternate slow and fast tasks that are dissimilar ("Walk the line slowly and then get down fast," "Draw slowly and then run fast"). These activities are effective if carried out to music of various speeds and intensities.

Games of this type are most effective if the child is given concrete evidence of just how slowly he is moving. Stop-watches, graphs, and other indications of increased success are vital to eliciting improvement. A similar important motivator can be the social approval of the teacher after the child has achieved increased success. Experimenters have also found that candy rewards or checkmarks that can be traded for toys also elicit better control of behavior in activities of this nature.

GAME 7   Do It Longer

Equipment: A number of 2 in. × 4 in. beams, 4, 6, or 8 ft. long, and/or lining tape, 2 in. wide; a large grassy area or a floor space.

Method: If both beams and tapes are available, children should be asked to walk both a beam and a tape to first determine what width and/or height truly challenges the child and requires close visual attention. When the material to be used is determined, construct gradually longer walking pathways, adding another beam, and then another (or another length of tape to the floor, and then another). Beams may be painted various colors, and beams of varying lengths may be used in the game. The children should be timed to determine how long they are walking (and attending) to the beam or line complexes of varying lengths.

Modifications: Other prolongation contests may be used, including asking children to balance a tennis ball for increased periods of time while holding waist high a balance platform consisting of a piece of plywood 2 ft. × 2 ft. square. Charts and graphs may be constructed by the children or the teacher to determine increased time and success at these and similar tasks. Children may be variously teamed in groups of timers, recorders, observers, and performers. Children who are well controlled may be paired with hyperactive youngsters to serve as role models in these types of games.

GAME 8   Say It . . . Do It . . . and Say It

Equipment: Large floor area, a coiled rope, or a group of hula-hoops. You may also use nylon boat line secured on an outdoor grass area with large nails placed in the ground. Use of nylon line of various colors in producing various kinds of agility courses of the type used in this game may help motivate students.

Method: First the object of the "game" is explained to the children. "You must jump over the ropes (hoops, etc.) you see before you without touching the rope with your feet." Before allowing the children to carry out this instruction, you should ask them to say, "I must jump over the ropes without touching them, and move just fast enough for good accuracy." Then they may begin (one at a time). While jumping, they may be first asked to hesitate, and then, depending upon their success, to make some statement regarding their progress and problems; for instance, "I did pretty well over the first two ropes, but then I got careless, and touched this last one. . . . I will continue, but will try to be more careful as I finish the course." As the children finish, they should be asked to make some kind of concluding statement, such as, "I did pretty well, it was fun, but I will try to move through it faster next time, taking greater care to jump over the ropes."

On trials that follow the first, the children should be encouraged to make statements aloud that reflect their true success or failure, to accurately assess their techniques, and to reward themselves in valid ways.

Modifications: Statements specific to the task of rope jumping may be gradually changed to more general self-talk statements, such as, "I should always plan what I will do before doing it." The use of a more mature child-model in a trial prior to exposing the hyperactive child to the task is highly effective in this type of game. The first "model" should be asked to engage in appropriate self-talk, using phrases that will be required later of the child with self-control problems. Children should be encouraged to compare each other's self-talk statements, for relevancy

with regard to their unique performance characteristics; for instance, more successful versus less successful trail or talk dealing with various kinds of errors—errors of omission (not negotiating a given rope), or errors of commission (jumping on a rope).

Finally, the child may be encouraged to phase out vocalized self-talk and imitate a teacher or another child model in the performance of thoughtful gestures before, during, or after the task. In this way overt heard self-talk may be gradually transformed into internal speech.

GAME 9   Maze Running and Talking

Equipment: A grassy area, containing a "people" maze delineated by lines, nailed to the ground with large nails (use nylon boat line or jump-rope rope); a desk area, containing a board, in which a raised finger maze is placed, or a pencil-and-paper maze with a conformation similar to, or identical to, that of the maze nailed on the ground.

The complexity of the mazes constructed should be compatible with the maturity of the children or youngsters participating.

Method: The object in this game (games) is to traverse the various mazes "as fast as you can." The finger mazes may be gone through with or without blindfold; the larger mazes may be traversed by running, jumping, skipping, or simply walking. As in Game 8, the children are asked prior to each trial to state what the object of the same is; for example, "I must run through this maze as fast as I can" or, "I must draw my pencil through this maze as fast as I can." During the traversal, if an error is committed, a self-talk statement might reflect the nature of this error, and its cause; for instance, "I went outside the line because I tried too hard, and went too fast." Finally, at the completion of the maze the children should be asked to state how successful they were, and what they might do next time to become more accurate or faster; for example, "I should be sure to make right turns more sharply next time, although I did do pretty well this time."

Modifications: This game may be engaged in by both normal children and by children who are visually impaired. Total times may be compared when both the sighted and visually impaired are competing if the sighted youngsters compete blindfolded. In the case of the larger maze, visually impaired children may crawl through, feeling the boundaries by hand, or the maze may be constructed of pathways delineated by plastic tubing placed in channels (2 to 3 ft. apart) and waist high, which they can feel when upright.

In this game, hyperactive children may be encouraged to copy or to model normal children. Both types of youngsters may be encouraged to reduce complete sentences to sentence fragments or whispers as they become able to traverse the mazes with increased speed and accuracy. Additionally, if the small finger mazes, shown below, contain the same patterns as do the larger maze, the children may be encouraged to first learn one (the larger or smaller one) and then proceed to the maze of the other size. This learning should also be accompanied by verbalizations reflecting the nature of the task. Verbal formulas should be practiced and said aloud, in order to facilitate both the specific learning tasks presented by these mazes as well as cognitive strategies in general.

Note: The more right angles in the mazes, the more amenable they are to reduction to verbal formulas.

CHILDREN WHO ARE TOO CALM

Although the introduction to the chapter mentioned that some children are too "dreamy" or "turned off" to work well in classroom, no space has been devoted to correcting their general behavioral problem.

However, it is far easier to arouse children than to calm them down. Most vigorous activities will accomplish this. Often apparently lethargic children suffer from hormonal or dietary deficiencies that should be thoroughly explored by the family physician. If medical attention does not correct the problem, the child might then be exposed to the vigorous activities mentioned above. One teacher with whom I am acquainted, for example, places the lethargic child on a small square board with a small board attached under the middle of the first board and asks the child to turn and to twist her body until she becomes more aware of what is happening around her.

SUMMARY AND OVERVIEW

The games and activities presented in this chapter were intended to be representative of the several types of methodologies that use movement and which may be used to heighten self-control and to prolong attention. These activities are by no means intended to represent a complete list of all the possible muscular exercises and movement games which it is possible to engage in within this context. Additionally, the games that have been described must be applied with patience and in various ways with various types of youngsters. Individual differences in muscular tensions that arise as the result of emotional upset often require various changes in the ways in which relaxation training is applied. Children who are nonverbal or display little language and children who have speech difficulties must be handled carefully if they are exposed to the games requiring self-talk.

Among the games not dealt with are sensory-motor stories of various kinds. Children may be told stories and required to act out slow, controlled movements in various ways. Within the framework of such active story telling it is often possible to slow down some of the more active of the group. The chapter also contained no games in which music or rhythms were used, though music and various tempos may be employed in useful ways within the game forms recommended here (Cratty 1981).

Contemporary research findings (often derived from studies conducted in public schools) suggest that the methods described, often combined with various kinds of meditational techniques and/or visual imagery, are useful in the reduction of stress in children and in heightening their self-control.[1] These types of activities may be interpolated in helpful ways throughout the schoolday—between stress-producing academic lessons, as well as within programs of motor development and physical education. I would very much like to learn of your experiences with these activities and about the games you design yourselves.

---

[1]Setterlind's 1983 study contains a bibliography containing over 400 investigations related to relaxation training in children (see Setterlind 1983).

BIBLIOGRAPHY

CAMERON, M.I., and ROBINSON, V.M.J. Effects of cognitive training on academic and task behavior of hyperactive children. *Journal of Abnormal Psychology*, 1980, *8*, 403-419.

CARTER, J.L., and SYNOLD, D. Effects of relaxation training upon handwriting quality. *Journal of Learning Disabilities*, 1974, *7*, 53-55.

CRATTY, B.J. Comparisons of verbal-motor performance and learning in serial memory tasks. *Research Quarterly*, 1963, *34*, 431-439.

————. Hyperactivity and its remediation. Chapter 12 in my *Remedial motor activity for children*. Philadelphia: Lea and Febiger, 1975.

————. Sequences of rhythm. Chapter 5 in B. J. Cratty, *Adapted physical education for handicapped children and youth*. Denver: Love Publishing, 1981.

CRATTY, B.J., and GIBSON, S. Motor planning and impulsivity in elementary school children. *Motorik*, in press, 1984.

CRATTY, B.J., and SZCZPANIK, M. *The effects of learning games upon academic abilities of learning disabled children*. Los Angeles: Dept. of Kinesiology, UCLA, Unpublished Monograph, 1970.

D'AMATO, G., and HERR, P.M. Inhibition of motor development in children with learning disabilities. *Perceptual and Motor Skills*, 1982, *54*, 1077-1078.

JACOBSON, E. *Progressive relaxation* (2nd ed.). Chicago: Univ. of Chicago Press, 1938.

JACOBSON, E., and LUFKIN, B. *Tension control in public schools: A research project in physical education*, Part 4. Chicago: Scientific Foundation, 1962.

MACCOBY, E., DOWLEY, E.M., and HAGEN, J.W. Activity level and intellectual functioning in normal pre-school children. *Child Development*, 1965, *36*, 761-769.

SETTERLIND, S. Relaxation training in schools. *Studies in Educational Sciences*, Univ. of Goteborg, Sweden, 1983, no. 43, 335.

CHAPTER 3

Basic Spatial Concepts

When children are born they initially demonstrate only a vague understanding of their spatial worlds. They deal at first with only the most rudimentary of spatial ideas, including differentiation between moving and stable stimuli, and between things that are a part of them and those that are not. Rather quickly however, with increased inspection and experience, more sophisticated visual perceptual concepts are acquired. Many of these early ideas are immediately transformed into useful behaviors. Inspection of the mouths of others quickly results in new sounds and lip movements, while the movement of objects and their appearance and disappearance also results in formation of new and important ideas about the continued existence of objects that may not be directly seen.

Between the second and fourth year, the child acquires verbal labels to attach to various ideas about configurations in space, and the location of objects in his visual world. The meanings of *up, down, into, around, in back of,* and like phrases are often discovered as the result of experiences at play during these formative years. The child learns to generalize between the same object that may appear in various forms or in different locations around the space field. Thus the child learns to recognize that a book may be large, small, or of various colors and that a car may be in motion or parked. These ideas about the constancy of objects in space, however, often begin to give the child trouble as he enters school. In the classroom children discover that objects called letters and numbers must be placed within highly rigid constraints before the teacher is made happy. An E must open to the right, they discover, while a wiggly line made into a M is not the same as apparently the same shape placed upside down and called a W!

Although theoretical arguments exist as to whether action on the part of the child is an *imperative* ingredient when learning about space[1], there is evidence that active games may enhance or accelerate the acquisition of many spatial concepts necessary for the child to function well in school and in life (Jeffrey 1958; Grabbard and Shea, 1979; Pharnes 1968).

This chapter presents a sampling of games that, played in sequential order, will aid the child to gain important spatial concepts. The majority of the activities concentrate upon geometric figures; however, the initial games in the chapter deal with more basic ideas, which must often precede learning about how space is bounded in the more common figures such as circles, squares, and the like. The final activities in the chapter point the child toward learning about and labelling both numbers and letters. Thus, this chapter may be considered an adjunct to those that follow (Chapters 5, 6, and 7).

Tasks designed to heighten the child's ability to recognize and name basic geometric patterns are found in most perceptual training programs. The research indicates that shortly after birth, infants can visually discriminate among circles, squares, and triangles, generally finding the triangle a more intriguing figure than the first two, as they spend more time looking at it.

Most training programs designed to teach children the differences between circles, squares, triangles, half-circles, diamonds, and the like use visual and tactual discrimination, as well as questions requiring the children to name the various patterns. The games found on the following pages add another dimension to pattern recognition; they involve some type of total body movement that accompanies the child's practice in the recognition and naming of the various figures.

Moreover, these games attempt to aid the child to attach verbal labels to each of the common figures.

Practice in naming geometric patterns can have several "side effects" that may later serve a child when attempting more complex learning problems. Several basic concepts may be taught through practice in pattern recognition and naming. For example:

(1) On learning the basic geometric patterns, their names, and their characteristics, a child can then be taught that letter forms can be constructed from them. She can be made to realize that two half-circles placed correctly can form a *B*, while one half-circle placed a certain way is a *b*; and that by modifying squares and rectangles in various ways, he can make *N*s, *M*s, *W*s, *L*s, *E*s, etc. Also, triangles make *A*s if one of their lines is moved upward slightly.

(2) Children taught to look for the basic characteristics of geometric figures are more likely to identify basic characteristics of letters; they are perhaps

[1]Works by Bower (1974), Cratty (1978), and others (Uhr 1966) in the bibliography at the end of this chapter illuminate these arguments.

less likely to be confused when shown an *A* in various styles of type or in script form. A triangle, for example, has the same characteristics whether on a horizontal plane, or placed on a wall, whether it is large or small. This general concept can serve a child in good stead when attempting to remember letter shapes appearing in various forms in various locations.

GAME 10 Up-and-Down . . . Back-and-Forth

Equipment: Blackboard, balance beams, mats, large pieces of butcher paper to write on, paper and pencil, desks, balls, etc.

Method: Children should be encouraged to find things they can do that involve going back and forth—running left to right and right to left—using their whole bodies. Children should observe each other doing "back and forth" things, including walking beams and ropes. Next, holding pencils to the butcher paper, they should make back and forth arm movements. The pencils will trace the pattern of the movements. This exercise should be done first with the paper flat on the floor and then with the paper on a wall. Finally the children should draw small back and forth lines on 8 in. × 10 in. paper while seated at a desk. Thus the children go from experience and observation of large (gross) movements to experience and observation of intermediate-size movements (limb movements while drawing on butcher paper), and

finally to experience and observation of small movements (the paper placed on the desk). In a similar manner, up and down movements should be first experienced with their whole bodies (or by throwing a ball straight up and then catching it) then through an intermediate motor experience involving drawing lines that go up and down on butcher paper, and finally through opportunities to draw up and down movements on paper while seated at a desk.

Discussion should take place outlining the purposes of the lesson, and discussing what similarities there are between the lines and spatial ideas contained in each subpart of the lesson.

Modifications: Children may start at the fine or intermediate level of movement, and proceed in turn to activities on the other levels. They should be encouraged to observe life's activities in the city streets and sidewalks, and identify what kinds of things go back and forth, up and down, etc. Finally a child/instructor may give verbal commands to another child or children, to move up and down (jump up, squat down), or move from side to side. Later, left–right labels may be applied to back and forth movements.

GAME 11   Slants and Curves

Equipment: Blackboard, desks, paper and pencil, balls, sliding board, ropes, slanted balance beams.

Method: As in Game 10, the object is to have children experience spatial concepts (this time of slanted and curved lines), first through total body movements, then through intermediate motor activities involving limb movements needed to inscribe large lines on butcher paper, then through small movements used when drawing slanted and curved lines while seated at a desk. Slanted total body experiences and observations can include holding a slanted rope while others jump over it at various heights; watching and experiencing a slide down a slanted board; and watching and experiencing a walk down a slanted balance beam. Curved experiences can include watching the arc of a ball thrown by one person to another, walking curved ropes placed on the ground, and the like. Intermediate motor activities, which should follow both slanted and curved movements of the total body, might include drawing large lines on the floor or on paper. Finally, transfer to a drawing task should be accomplished by placing the children at desks, and using paper which is 8 in. × 10 in. in size.

Modifications: Children, if they are able, may be encouraged to draw pictures with various slanted lines, and to identify slanted lines they see in the community, such as in signs. Later the children may be asked to reproduce or/and identify letters that have slanted components.

GAME 12   Crossing Lines

Equipment: Lining tape that may be placed on or nailed to the ground, ropes, dowels 3 ft. to 4 ft. long and 1/2 in. or less in diameter, blackboard, butcher paper, desks, and pencils and paper.

Method: Children should be informed that today they are having a lesson on lines that cross. Next they should be given "crossing experiences" walking over lines taped to the floor in patterns that involve crossing. Sticks that are crossed on the ground may be jumped over in various ways. Other movement experiences may use stimuli and/or actions that involve crossing. Next the children should be exposed to opportunities that permit them to draw crossed lines using limb movements on large pieces of paper placed on the floor. Large crossing (movement) lines may be drawn on the blackboard. Finally, as in Games 10 and 11, the children should be seated, and should attempt to draw crossing lines on 8 in. × 10 in. paper. This final drawing can include attempts to make geometric figures and letters, thus leading into the more advanced games contained in this chapter, as well as to the games involving letter recognition and production in the chapters that follow.

Modifications: If they are able, the children may be asked to invent games with patterns that require the children to run in pathways that cross. Moreover, crossing lines may be used to initiate pattern drawing. Finally, clay may be employed to form letters that have intersecting and/or crossing lines. Clay letters then may be transformed into written/printed letters.

GAME 13   See and Match

Equipment: Patterns on squares, blackboard.

Method: Place two pattern squares at a time in front of the child; draw one of the patterns on blackboard; ask child to jump or hop into correct one, given two choices.

Modifications: Give three squares to choose from, then four, then five. Erase pattern after it is shown to child, and then ask him to jump or hop into proper square containing matching pattern.

GAME 14   Jump and Say

Equipment: Squares with geometric figures on them.

Method: Children jump on each square in order, saying what geometric figure each one is as they land on it. Mix up order of squares after every few children jump on them.

Modifications: If child is correct in two or three, have her draw these on blackboard. Observers check accuracy of children jumping and make corrections when necessary. Have children attempt to change geometric figures on blackboard to standard block letters—making triangle into an *A*, half-circles into a *B*, half-circle into a *C*.

GAME 15   Hear and Jump

Equipment: Squares containing geometric figures.

Method: Geometric figure is called out while child tries to find it and jump or hop into proper square. Other children check and correct accuracy.

Modifications: Speed up rate of calling. If child is correct, he can draw it on the board and then change geometric figure into letter. Delays of increasing duration can be inserted after figure is called and before response can be made to prolong auditory memory. Children can work in pairs, one calling and the other jumping.

GAME 16   See and Throw

Equipment: Squares containing geometric figures, small bean bags (bags can be on strings for handicapped children), blackboard.

Method: Geometric figure is drawn on board and then child tries to find it among several and to throw bean bag into correct one. Other observing children check accuracy.

Modifications: Child can throw first and then say which geometric figure bag landed in. Handicapped child, in wheelchair, can retrieve bag via string and repeat without help from teacher. Child can be given geometric figure auditorily and then try to throw into proper one without any visual comparison on board. Child can be given capital letter on board and then asked to throw it into geometric figure that makes up the letter (*D* = half-circle, *Q* = circle, *N* = square).

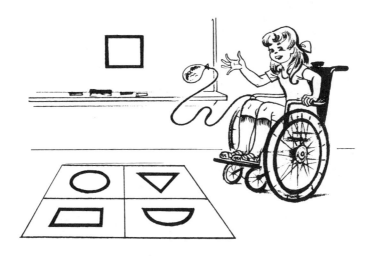

GAME 17   Go and Get It

Equipment: Blackboard, squares containing geometric figures.

Method: Children line up with squares placed between them. The name of one figure is called out. Two children who are then touched by teacher at same time race to see who can retrieve square first and bring it back to line. Winner can draw it on blackboard.

Modifications: Figure is written on board rather than called out. Letter is called out and child must retrieve the geometric figure that will form it with modifications. Children on two teams may be numbered one to five; then teacher may call "two-rectangle," meaning that the number-two children on each team must see who can get the rectangle square first.

GAME 18   Cut and Find

Equipment: Scissors, cardboard, blackboard, and squares containing geometric figures.

Method: Children first see figure on blackboard and then cut it out of cardboard and find it on the proper square. The child should note similar characteristics of cardboard figure and the one found on the square (number of sides, corners, and so on).

Modifications: On finding the proper square, the child can see how many things she can do to it (hop on it, run around it, jump over it). She also can count sides or corners of both figures to check accuracy. The handicapped child can throw a bean bag into the proper square.

GAME 19   Big Things and Little Things

Equipment: Lining tape, cardboard, scissors, blackboard, squares containing geometric figures.

Method: Illustrate that the same figure can be made larger or smaller. Start with jumping into squares containing figures; jump and say what they are; then ask children to either "make larger ones" (with lining tape on playground or gymnasium floor) or smaller ones (drawing on blackboard or cutting them out of cardboard). After this is done, even smaller ones may be cut out or drawn or larger ones can be made on floor, and games can be played in these larger ones (for example, three-base game on triangle).

Modifications: Larger and smaller figures may be placed just on floor or just on blackboard, drawing same figures of increasing or decreasing size. Discussion should take place concerning characteristics of each geometric figure. Big and little letters may be drawn on blackboard.

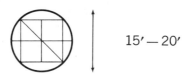

15′ — 20′

GAME 20   Jump and Tape

Equipment: Squares containing geometric figures, yellow lining tape 2 in. wide, blackboard.

Facilities: Playground or gymnasium with yellow-lined, large geometric figures of all types.

Method: Child draws figure asked for on a blackboard, runs to proper square containing same figure, jumps into it, and then finds even larger figure on playground on gym floor. If it is not there, he may then use lining tape and make his own figure on a playground or on the gym floor.

Modifications: Child may be asked to invent games on one of the larger geometric figures. He may be asked to do three or more things within one of the figures (to walk their edges, count their sides, and then to modify figures into letters using additional pieces of lining tape for example, changing rectangle into *M, N, L,* or *H*).

GAME 21   Find It in the Maze

Equipment: Complex figure, containing all standard geometric figures as shown; squares containing geometric figures; blackboard.

Method: Child is shown a single figure or it is called out, and then she must run through the corresponding figure within the complex figure maze.

Modifications: Child must first jump into square containing figure, say what it is, and then run through it on larger complex pattern. Child may run through all figures on complex pattern, calling them out as she moves. Child first runs through figure and then draws it on board, and then perhaps changes it into letter shape on board. Child in wheelchair may ask partner to push her through proper pathways while child gives directions to partner.

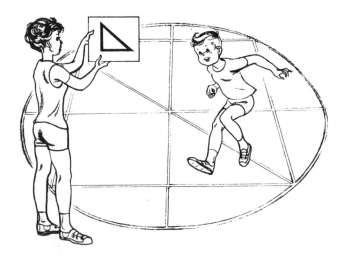

GAME 22   Find It and Do It, in Order

Equipment: Squares containing geometric figures.

Method: Arrange squares in half-circle; ask children to jump or to do something in each and then ask other children to copy them; use two, three, four, and then five squares in this manner. Child may do "his own thing" in each square and then either repeat these actions or request another

child in the class to copy them exactly; first child acts as evaluator. Each time a square is jumped on, it must be named (circle, half-circle, and so on).

Modifications: Use a ball and do something to each square with a ball (roll it over, bounce it, dribble it around). Call out geometric figure when each is approached.

GAME 23   Left Things and Right Things

Equipment: Square containing geometric figures, blackboard.

Method: Children jump, hop on one foot, or do something to each square when encountered. They both identify square's geometric figure and also say whether they are doing a "right" thing or a "left" thing (hopping into it with a right foot, jumping around it to the left side).

Modifications: Handicapped child in wheelchair may be asked whether her bean bag landed to the left or right of the center of each square aimed at, as well as being asked the name of the geometric figure in each square. Children may observe and evaluate each other's efforts ("Is it really to the left (or right)?" "Is it truly a circle?" "Is it truly a half-circle with which you are dealing?").

GAME 24   Up and Down in Space

Equipment: Blackboard, mats, balls, ropes, hoops, and other miscellaneous playground equipment; blackboard, chalk.

Method: Children are shown various configurations in pairs on the blackboard, starting with ↑ ↓. They are asked to attach an up or down movement to the configuration, indicating the direction the blackboard symbol seems to go. New symbol-to-movement codes may be formulated by the children, illustrating an up-or-down "thing" with a ball reflecting an up or down symbol; for instance, ∨ could stand for throwing a ball up, while ∧ could represent dropping a ball down (or bouncing it).

Modifications: A ball may be used, and either dropped to a down symbol or tossed up and recaught when an up symbol is used. Combining responses also may be used with the placement of the blackboard near a piece of outdoor apparatus; that is, an up symbol could mean to climb higher, while a down symbol might mean "descend."

GAME 25   Left and Right in Space

Equipment: Blackboard, mats, balls, ropes and the like.

Method: Leading out of Game 23, children are asked to respond by moving to the left or right by responding to various configurations on the blackboard that have asymmetrical properties. For example, ⊣ could initially stand for moving to the left (or using the left hand in something), while ⊢ could represent a movement to right, or some movement of the right hand. Other symbols may then be used, including those which represent the confusing pairs *b–d* and *p–q*, thus leading to the letter identification qualities seen in chapters that follow. Thus a symbol-movement coding system is learned, to emphasize this nature of assymetrical letter/symbols to be encountered later.

Aiding the child to identify these kinds of asymmetrical symbols, letters, and configurations may be accomplished by having the youngster reach out and touch each side of such a symbol with the appropriate hand; for instance, have the child respond to such instructions as, "reach with your left hand to the *d*, and tell me which side is the curved part of the *d*" or, "now reach out to the blackboard with your right hand, and tell me which side of the *E* is open."

Modifications: Ball games may be played using asymmetrical symbols to trigger throwing responses, i.e., a "left" symbol means throw the ball to your left (or to the target on your left) while a "right" symbol means throw the ball to your right. Later, children may be exposed to entire words, which may or may not match a key word relative to the correct right/left placement of letters. For example, if the word written second (*WAS*) is the same as (*SAW*) placed on the board, the child might respond. If not, no response may have been required. In this way, simple left/right concepts are translated into understanding the complex left/right arrangement of letters in words.

GAME 26   Lots of Things

Equipment: Squares containing geometric figures, cardboard, scissors, bean bag with string attached.

Method: Children cut out all geometric figures into sizes about 3 in. × 3 in. While holding the △ or □ in their hands, they attempt to jump to correct matching square holding same figure in the correct order (as each one is landed in, child shuffles another one to the top in his hand-held packet, finds its match by jumping in it, and then places another small square on the top, finds it, and continues).

Modifications: Child in wheelchair can shuffle them in his lap and then try to throw bean bag into correct square. After retrieving it, a second and a third pattern can be thrown.

GAME 27   Bodies and Shapes

Equipment: Large matted area, blackboard, ropes, balls, tape, sticks, and the like.

Methods: Children are encouraged to work in pairs. One of each pair is asked to lie down (or stand) in the form of one of the basic geometric shapes previously studied (squares, triangles, etc). Their partners are asked first to observe, then both to draw and to identify verbally the shape that their partner's body has formed. The partners may then reverse roles. This game may be extended into those ideas necessary to begin to form letter recognition and number recognition concepts. That is, the child forming the letter may be asked to form one that is "the same on both sides" (a symmetric letter, such as *o i u y*, as well as those that are not the same on both sides, including such asymmetrical letters as *d, f, g, k, q, z, x.*

Modifications: Children beginning to acquire advanced spatial concepts needed in letter and number recognition, including normal youngsters entering school, as well as atypical children who are older chronologically, may also benefit from beginning to spell out simple words with more than one child involved.

SUMMARY AND OVERVIEW

This chapter contains games and activities suggestive of a general sequence of necessary percepts and concepts about space and about various ways in which space may be primitively bounded in the form of geometric figures. Although the games begin with those involving relatively simple concepts of up-down, back-forth (taught through experience with horizontal lines and movement), as well as slanted-curved and crossing lines in space, the teacher or parent may have to begin with activities that are even more basic when working with the very young or the very handicapped youngster. For example, games involving motor responses to such directions as "come here" or "go there" must accompany activities that encourage the understanding of "location" words in the language such as "over," "under," "beside," "behind," "into," and "on top of." Games of this nature may be played with large boxes, permitting the child and teacher to locate themselves in various ways while talking about their locations; tables may be used in a similar way.

The sequences reflected in the games within the chapter move from activities intended to teach about spatial directions and accompanying concepts to actions needed to place verbal labels on common geometric figures, including triangles, squares, and the like. The final parts of the chapter provide lead-in experiences to activities within succeeding chapters dealing with letter and number identification and recognition. Thus the final games in this section deal with more precise spatial dimensions than were the subject of the initial games (10, 11, and 12). These last activities (Games 23 through 27) help the child conceptualize about up and down in space as well as about important left-right ideas about space, concepts vital to the initial and correct identification of asymmetrical letters and numbers.

BIBLIOGRAPHY

BOWER, T.G.R. *Development in infancy.* San Francisco: W.H. Freeman & Company, Publishers, 1985.

CRATTY, B.J. *Perceptual and motor development in infants and children.* Englewood Cliffs, NJ: Prentice-Hall, 1985.

GRABBARD, C.P., and SHEA, C.H. Influence of movement activities on shape recognition and retention. *Perceptual and Motor Skills*, 1979, *48*, 116-118.

JEFFREY, W.E. Variables in early discrimination learning: Motor responses in training a left-right discrimination. *Child Development*, 1958, *29*, 269-275.

PHARNES, J.S. *The relationship between whole body movement and the retarded child's ability to learn selected geometric forms.* M.S. thesis, University of North Carolina, 1968.

UHR, L., Ed. *Pattern recognition.* New York: John Wiley, 1966.

CHAPTER 4

Remembering Things

Remembering a series of items is an everyday necessity. Phone numbers must be memorized, spelling and counting must be mastered, and directions must be remembered.

A great deal is known about people's ability to remember verbal information. Lists of nonsense syllables have been the subject of innumerable learning studies published in psychological journals since before the turn of the twentieth century. Within recent years, the ability of children to learn and to retain information of various kinds has been afforded increasing attention. My colleagues and I found that practice in remembering correctly a series of movements performed by another child and in repeating these movements contributed positively to children's ability to remember a series of pictures, words, and letters. In this same study we found high-to-moderate correlations among scores in serial memory tasks regardless of what was to be remembered.

Our observations have further suggested that it is easier for a child to perform a series of movements and then to remember and to again perform these same movements in the same order than it is for a child to observe another and then to copy her movements in the same order. We have also noted that the type of game outlined in this chapter is highly motivating to children. They request this kind of task again and again, and we have often used it as a reward for good work at the end of the learning sessions.

It will usually be found that movements toward the middle of a series will be harder for a child to duplicate than the first and final movements in the series. A similar phenomenon has been noted when researching the retention of pieces of verbal information.

As can be seen when scanning the following games, several purposes can be served. For example, several games employ numbers, letters, and geometric figures. Other games test a child's ability to remember a series of locations rather than a series of movements made in a given order.

It is also apparent on examining the games that activities of this nature can be made extremely difficult. By requiring children to perform, to remember a number of things in each configuration, and/or to remember both movements and locations in order, their intellects will be severely taxed.[1]

The games in this chapter also reflect new trends in the findings of studies about how children learn to remember better. These investigations first resulted in outcomes that pointed out that as children mature they begin to think in more precise ways about how they are to remember various kinds of information. For example, even four-year-olds are able to evidence various kinds of useful strategies that help them to remember. A young child of this age who is informed that later he will be asked to remember an object's location in a room will be seen to stare intently at the object's location. In the next two years children become able to predict rather accurately just how much material they are likely to remember, as well as how much material they are likely to retain at a later time (Flavell, Friedrich, and Hoyt 1970).

Recently, investigators have used developmental information about how children learn how to remember as they grow older to formulate memory-training programs. The preliminary results have been promising. Asnarow and Meichenbaum (1979) found, for example, that kindergarten children trained in self-instruction learned more and remembered more a week later. Specific kinds of mental rehearsal techniques were provided in this investigation. Brown, Campione, and Barclay (1978) obtained similar findings when evaluating the effects of self-taught strategies for memorization provided to retarded children.

It is for this reason that several of the games that follow not only provide variations in memory tasks but also suggest ways in which the child may learn how to remember. This kind of meta-cognitive training, also treated in Chapter 2, provides, it is believed, one of the more important outcomes of practicing the activities that follow. Learning about and practicing methods to enhance memory are effective ways to provide experiences in these movement memory games that will transfer to tasks requiring memorization found in a variety of classroom subjects.

Most pertinent to the focus of this text has been work carried out in the early 1980s that specifically points to the facilitation effects of memory training using movement tasks. For example, Saltz (1981) found that movement facilitated the memory of sentences containing various "action themes." When children were told to "act out" such sentences as, "The fireman ran toward the burning building," or "The soldiers marched into battle," they remembered more later than if they were not asked to move as the sentences were presented the first time. In addition, he found that movement responses accomplished more retention in this type of task than did asking the children merely to visualize the actions. In a similar study, Levin (1976) also found that the

---

[1]Tasks involving serial memory are usually found in IQ tests.

memory of toys was facilitated if they were grasped and acted upon, rather than if they were not handled. These and earlier studies in this same topic area seem to indicate that somehow the child *encodes* and stores information in a more vivid and useful way when a movement has been attached to a concept, object, or idea. Movement-paired thoughts may thus be more easily retrievable from both short-term and long-term memory than thoughts that are not stored in the same vivid manner.

Using movements to teach memory strategies has been suggested in several games that follow. Again, corroborative data is available that suggests the desirability of this approach. Paris, Newman, and Nevey (1982), for example, found that teaching a variety of strategies to enhance memory, using children from 7 to 8 years old, facilitated later retention. Most important, however, they found that if the children were made to *understand the rationale* underlying each of the memory (or mnemonic) strategies used, even more retention took place. The strategies that aided the children's understanding included (a) rehearsal; (b) grouping information; and (c) *blocked recall*, trying to remember content momentarily with the eyes closed, and other memory tools.

Considerable variations will be found in the reactions of groups of younger children when they are introduced to various ways to enhance memory (Meichenbaum and Asnarow 1979). Most authorities believe, however, that children who are better able to engage in these kinds of meta-cognitive behaviors are better classroom learners (Flavell 1979).

The games in this chapter include various kinds of memory strategies. These include verbalizing what is to be remembered, visual rehearsal, and others. The transfer of these strategies to classroom learning tasks should be carried out carefully, so that the participating children are able to understand clearly just how these memory strategies may be applied in a relatively wide variety of learning situations.

Although the illustrations generally show the use of two-dimensional obstacles (lines and configurations on a flat surface), these same games can be played using three-dimensional obstacles (tires, boxes, bars, tree trunks, and the like). It should also be noted that the obstacles, whether two- or three-dimensional, are usually arranged in a semicircular pattern. In this manner it is possible, we believe, to maintain better class control than would be the case if children, when finishing their "trip," ended up a linear distance away from their starting point. Arranged in this way, the games also provide a better view to the observing children.

Serial memory ability is closely related to perceptual span. The latter quality involves the ability to quickly and accurately count and/or otherwise identify a group of configurations when only given a brief time to inspect them. It is believed that innumerable qualities can be enhanced using these interesting games; many more modifications are possible than are contained in the following pages.

In investigations conducted in selected Catholic elementary schools in Los Angeles, practice in the type of serial memory tasks described in this chapter was found to have several outcomes: (a) The children's ability to remember a series of movements changed from an average of slightly over three to almost six by the end of the semester; (b) Their ability to remember and to repeat a series of numbers, given verbally, in correct order showed similar improvement; (c) Their ability to remember and to place in correct order a series of pictures presented visually also improved significantly, as contrasted with the performance of control groups who had no practice in "movement" serial memory tasks. Most important is the fact that the two serial memory tasks described in (b) and (c) were not engaged in during the semester-long training period.

GAME 28   Where Did I Visit?

Equipment: Lining tape, squares containing geometric figures placed as shown.

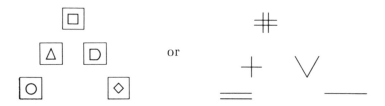

Methods: A demonstrating child is asked to "visit (go to) one of the figures," (using either set), while observing children are asked to remember where the demonstrator has gone. The demonstrating child returns to the group, and observers are then asked, one at a time, to go the the same place the demonstrator has gone. This game is continued, rotating demonstrators from among the observers and adding "places"—from 1, to 2, 3, 4, and more. Thus the problem becomes one of remembering not only locations, but the order in which they have been "visited" by the first demonstrator.

Modifications: Added variety may be obtained by asking the demonstrators to go the locations in different ways; for instance, by running, hopping, or skipping. Thus the problem now becomes one of remembering not only location and order, but the movement pattern used to travel to each location. Variations of this game may be provided for handicapped children who lack locomotor skills. Wheelchair skills may be demonstrated, to give one example.

GAME 29 Say, Think, and Go

Equipment: Draw the figures (shown below) containing pictures; blackboard may also be used.

Method: A child is asked to go to one of the figures containing pictures. Observing children are told that they should remember where the demonstrating child has gone. Moreover, they should be told to *say* out loud, "I must remember where _____ has gone," before the demonstration. After the demonstration, they should be told to say out-loud, "_____ has gone to the cow" (or to whatever location has been visited). More and more locations may be added, with demonstrators and observer/performers rotated. As in Game 28, children may vary how they "visit" each figure. However, the method of traveling to the figures should be added to the vocalization practice used by the observers; for instance, "Johnny went to the house, skipping."

Modifications: Children may contrast the quality of their memory with and without vocalization as part of their efforts to retain. Other modifications include reducing vocalization to whispered sentences or to sentence fragments—for example, "John skips to the cow!" becomes "John, skip, cow"—and later to single words as cues. Verbalization either before or after observers try to duplicate demonstrator may be contrasted for efficiency. Verbalization of errors and correction of errors may also be attempted; for instance, "I remembered the place—the cow—but I forgot how to go there—skipping."

GAME 30   Repeat Myself

Equipment: Lining tape as shown, lines about 2 ft. long, figures about 2 ft. apart.

Method: Child does one to four things to figure and then tries to repeat exactly the same things herself. Observing teacher or another child evaluates the accuracy of her efforts. The child may hop, jump, run around, jump into, and so forth.

Modifications: May do movements backward (jump backward, sideways, with one foot, turning movements). Figures may be added. Other modifications may include having the demonstrating child describe the movement, or movements, verbally either before or after she performs them (it). Contrasts may be made between self-memory with and without attempts to verbalize what has taken place.

GAME 31   Picture It!

Equipment: The configurations shown for Game 32, a blackboard, ropes, balls, sticks, and the like.

Method: Children are asked to observe while a demonstrator executes a single movement (or posture) at one location. Observing children are then asked one at a time to first close their eyes and try to "turn on a television picture" of the movement they have just seen, and must perform next. Then they are asked to perform the movement. This should be continued for two or more movements, with visualization used between each trial as a memory technique.

Modifications: Children may be asked to perform with and without interpolated attempts at visualization. Discussions of how "clear" each of their

"pictures" is could lead to discovery of individual differences in visual imagery used. Contrasts may be made of memory without and with visualization. Words or pictures (or both) may be drawn on the board, with visualization used before attempts to remember the pictures or words. Discussions about what is best pictured and what may be best described in words might focus attention upon when visualization techniques are best. Visual imagery and verbalization (as used in Game 30) may be combined or contrasted as memory aids.

GAME 32 Tell Me Where I Went

Equipment: Squares containing geometric patterns or tape making configurations similar to those shown in Games 28 and 30.

Method: Child visits (hops or jumps there) each of three or four figures, not necessarily in order. Second observing child either informs the first child where he went as he tries to repeat himself or verbally informs a third child where the first child "visited" and in what order.

Modifications: Number of configurations visited can be increased; what was done in each may be made different—hop in one, jump in a second, and so on. Order can be changed after each turn.

GAME 33   Ball Things

Equipment: Lining tape or squares containing geometric patterns arranged in semicircle as shown in Games 31 and 32, using three to seven patterns or squares; two or three 8-in. diameter rubber playground balls.

Method: A child does something with a ball in each configuration (or square) in order (bounces it in 1, rolls it over 2, and so on). Second observing child tries to repeat what was done, in the same order, at each configuration. First child observes him and instructs him when errors are observed.

Modifications: A third child can continue to act as an observer and either correct the evaluator or instruct other children in exactly what the first child did. This instruction can be verbal (to aid in language development), can be demonstrated, or can be both demonstrated and described.

GAME 34   Add One

Equipment: Serial memory configurations as shown in Games 31 and 32, composed either of squares containing letters, numbers, geometric figures, or figures made of tape as shown.

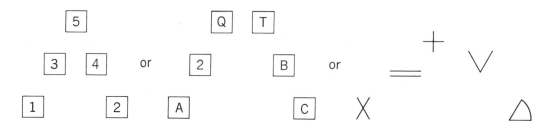

Method: First child does something to one configuration; second child repeats what first child did and adds another to the second figure; third child copies first two movements on first two configurations and then adds her own movement to the third.

Modifications: May use ball; do a left or right thing; simply visit one, two, or three or more stations in an irregular order (not necessarily starting with first one to the right, with the second and subsequent children trying to remember where previous ones visited and then adding visits of their own).

GAME 35   Divide and Remember

Equipment: Balls, ropes, figures like those used in Games 31 and 32.

Method: Demonstrating children require observers to remember an increasing number of movements among several figures (eight or more maximum). When a "top off" is reached (that is, no more movements can be remembered), a discussion should take place concerning how the movement-places may be divided (or "chunked"), so that they can be better remembered. The game should continue, then, and the memory of six, seven, or more places and movements may be enhanced by doing three movements with a ball, and then three movements without a ball in order to remember a total of six movements, for example. Or three jumping movements and three hopping movements may be combined so a total of six movements are remembered.

Modifications: This division (or chunking) of things to be remembered may be combined with the visualization and verbal rehearsal techniques described in previous games. More important, this general principle of organizing long lists (or much material) to be remembered into smaller parts should be discussed and practiced within a classroom. Thus, when the children are confronted with letters, words, multiplication tables, chemistry formulae, and the like, they may employ these same memory strategies.

GAME 36   Left and Right

Equipment: Serial memory squares or taped figures as shown in Games 32 and 33.

Method: First child does a left thing or right thing in each of four to six figures (jumps with left foot, runs around second to the right) and is asked to tell whether he is going to the left or the right. Observing teacher or another child (should have a mental age above nine years) tells whether responses are correct.

Modifications: Observing child may attempt to repeat in correct order the responses of the first performing child. Observing child may try to tell a third child what the first child did, as the third child attempts to duplicate first's responses correctly. A follow-the-leader game might be started, with each child attempting to do what the child ahead of him does.

GAME 37   Arrange and Show

Equipment: Tape, squares containing letters, numbers, or geometric figures.

Method: Children are allowed to place tape or squares in the order they decide upon. They then jump into them, calling out their characteristics if they are letter, number, or geometric-figure squares. They then mix them up and see if observing children can place them in the same order and jump into them the same way.

Modifications: Interpolate taped figures between squares that are movable; keep taped figures intact. Do more than one thing to each square; visit squares in different orders (not in the order they are placed next to each other).

GAME 38   Associations

Equipment: Ropes, balls, sticks, blackboard, and figures as used in Games 31 and 32.

Method: Children should be asked to watch an observer execute a movement in a given location, with or without a ball, stick, or rope. They should then be asked first to (a) associate the movement with something else that is similar and then (b) to try to duplicate it. For example, the first child might stand on one foot, and the observing children (or child) might be asked to say out loud, or to themselves (herself), "John stands like a stork." Perhaps the movement involves jumping, in this case the observer may be prompted to say (subvocally or overtly), "Jane jumps like a frog." This associational learning may be continued for two, three, or more figures. The children should be asked to experiment with verbalizing associations, and/or with visualizing associations; for instance "Picture Donald bouncing his ball on the back of a turtle."

Modifications: Contrasts in memory may be made with and without either verbal or visual associations. "Top-off points" (item limits of memory span) may be experimented with concerning how many things may be remembered with and without visual or verbal associations. Children could compete to see how absurd or logical the associations they form can be. Discussions of how associations of this kind may aid in the memorization and retention of classroom tasks may be coupled with actual practice in classroom tasks.

GAME 39   Many Things

Equipment: Letter, number, or geometric squares arranged as shown in Game 34 or taped figures; balls, ropes, and so on.

Method: Child does more than one thing at each configuration and visits from two to four configurations. Observing child attempts to duplicate order of visits, plus what was done at each configuration or square. The child might do a ball thing and a jumping thing at each configuration or square or perhaps three things at each stop.

Modifications: Child might try to duplicate his own things. Observing child might try to verbalize and tell a third child what the first child did at each stop. Children may experiment with other memory aids described in previous games including chunking (or dividing material to be learned), visualization, and verbalization, as well as the associational practices explained in Game 38.

SUMMARY AND OVERVIEW

Serial memory games have been found to be highly motivating and helpful to children. The combinations of games may be used to enhance memory, left-right discrimination, geometric-figure, letter, and number identification. Observational skills as well as language skills may be incorporated by the imaginative teacher into some of the activities described. Increasing difficulty can be introduced by having a child try to remember an increasing number of things or by requiring a child to remember and duplicate complex movements made by another child.

   These games and strategies represent only a brief introductory look at the possible ways in which teachers and parents may aid children to remember better. Memory is the basis for more complex and exotic intellectual processes.

A good memory provides the data, the basic "stuff," that may then be used with new and creative problems or may be analyzed or synthesized in a variety of ways.

These games are intended to provide not only happy series of movement "things" to remember, but also to enable a teacher or parent to help children to discover useful memory strategies. Thus the use of visualization techniques, the processes of "chunking," of forming associations, and of vocalizing about what is to be remembered should not only aid the child to learn academic tasks better, but provide a foundation for the activities in chapters that follow this one (Piaget 1962).

Various memorization processes have been only briefly touched upon in this chapter. The reader who wishes to pursue these potentially valuable ways of learning should consult the references that follow (Bruner 1964; Paris, Newman, and Nevey 1982).

BIBLIOGRAPHY

ASNAROW, J.R., and MEICHENBAUM, D. Verbal rehearsal and serial recall: The mediational training of kindergarten children. *Child Development*, 1979, *50*, 1173-1177.

BROWN, A., CAMPIONE, J., and BARCLAY, C.R. *Training self-checking routines for estimating test readiness: Generalization from list learning to prose recall.* Unpublished manuscript, Univ. of Illinois, 1978.

BROWN, A., CAMPIONE, J., and MURPHY, P. Maintenance and generalization of trained metamnemonic awareness of educable retarded children. *Journal of Experimental Child Psychology*, 1977, *24*, 191-211.

BRUNER, J.S. The course of cognitive growth. *American Psychologist*, 1964, *19*, 1-15.

COHEN, R., SCHLESER, A., and MEYERS, R. Self-instructions: Effects of cognitive level and active rehearsal. *Journal of Experimental and Child Psychology*, 1981, *32*, 65-76.

FLAVELL, J.H. Metacognition and cognitive monitoring. *American Psychologist*, 1979, *34*, 906-911.

FLAVELL, J.H., BEACH, D., and CHINSKY, J. Spontaneous verbal rehearsal in a memory task as a function of age. *Child Development*, 1966, *37*, 283-299.

FLAVELL, J.H., and WELLMAN, H. Metamemory. In R. Kail and J. Hagen (Eds.), *Perspectives on the development of memory and cognition.* Hillsdale, NJ: Lawrence Erlbaum, 1977.

KEENEY, T., CANNIZZO, S., and FLAVELL, J.H. Spontaneous and induced verbal rehearsal in a recall task. *Child Development*, 1967, *38*, 953-966.

LEVIN, J.R.   What have we learned about maximizing what children learn? In J.R. Levin and L.L. Allen (Eds.), *Cognitive learning in children*. New York: Academic Press, 1976.

MEICHENBAUM, D., and ASNAROW, J.R.   Cognitive-behavioral modification and metacognitive development: Implications for the classroom. In P. Kendall and S. Hollon (Eds.), *Cognitive-behavioral interventions: Theory, research and procedures*. New York: Academic Press, 1979.

PARIS, S.G., NEWMAN, R.S., and MCVEY, K.A.   Learning the functional significance of mnemonic actions: A microgenetic study of the strategy of acquisition. *Journal of Experimental Child Psychology*, 1982, 34, 490-509.

PIAGET, J.   *Play, dreams, imitation*. New York: Norton, 1962.

REESE, H.   Verbal mediation as a function of age. *Psychological Bulletin*, 1962, 59, 502-509.

SALTZ, E.   Let's pretend: The role of motoric imagery in memory for sentences and words. *Journal of Experimental Child Psychology*, 1982, 34, 77-92.

SALTZ, E., and DONNENWERTH-NOLAN, S.   Does motoric imagery facilitate memory for sentences? A selective interference test. *Journal of Verbal Learning and Verbal Behavior*, 1981, 20, 322-332.

CHAPTER 5

Numbers and Mathematics

The activities in this chapter are intended to supplement and enhance classroom exercises that introduce children to numbers and develop their abilities to deal with them. Games in this section also deal with the manipulation of numerical concepts in the form of basic mathematical operations, including addition, subtraction, multiplication, and division.

Physical activity can be useful in learning quantitative concepts and operations (Owen 1976; Ross 1970; Humphrey 1972). Movement requires space. Quantity is vividly portrayed to a learner as she jumps a given distance—an amount of space that can be accurately measured with a precise number of units.

Quantitative concepts, including rudimentary counting, are encountered early in the life of an infant. By the third month, the child often echoes precisely the number of syllables he hears emanating from a mother or father hovering over the crib. When a parent says, "Da ... da ... da," the same number of syllables are often repeated by the maturing infant well before the sixth month of life. Rhythmic play soon begins to lead to counting within the second and third year of life. Counting is an imperative basis for more sophisticated mathematical operations (Hendrickson 1979). After counting has been practiced, new situations requiring ideas about quantity may be learned (Wang, Resnick, and Boozer 1971). Indeed, it has been found that children whose sensory-awareness of their fingers is poor often have problems using these same fingers when trying to learn to count and to engage in more complex mathematical operations.[1]

[1] Two main theoretical approaches have been proposed to explain how mathematical abilities develop in children: one based upon the writings of Piaget (1952), and the second upon a model proposed by those interested in information theory (Simon 1969). The enterprising reader is encouraged to consult these references.

Newer methods for teaching mathematics employ the manipulation of sets of objects. It has been found that children as young as four may be taught to subtract and to add using this approach (Groen and Resnick 1977; Brush 1978). It has also been found that word problems may be solved by pre-school children well before they receive formal instruction in subtraction or addition. Indeed these kinds of problems, it has been found, provide a good basis for the later written symbolization of quantitative concepts (Hamrick 1979).

Mathematical games have been reported for many decades. Marie Montessori, for example, taught mathematics by grouping children in various ways and then asking her young charges to count the numbers of children in various groups as they were divided and combined. She used children as units in math games. Some of the games in this chapter use that same approach, while others employ Arabic numerals (Humphrey 1966, 1968).

The concrete experiences offered by active movement games have been used recently to inculcate math operations and concepts in the minds of hard-of-hearing youngsters whose internal speech may limit their ability to conceptualize in quantitative ways. I recently designed a "mathematics playground," containing twelve stations, in a state school for the deaf. This approach, combined with a pretend "village" consisting of numerous "stores," comprised the main program of mathematics within this California institution.

For the most part, attempts to translate an entire elementary school mathematics program into active games are more successful than attempts to teach an entire reading program in the same way (Ginsburg 1977). The abstractions found in language are not always amenable to a "movement-teaching-approach," while the concrete operations found in the beginning math lessons can be translated into games with relative ease. At the same time the activities that follow are meant to supplement, not to replace, traditional classroom lessons. It is hoped that they are useful in this respect.

GAME 40   Swing Ball Count

Equipment: A playground ball, 8 in. in diameter, suspended overhead from a line 4-6 ft. in length.

Method: Two or more children are arranged so that they may contact the swinging ball with their hands as it is pushed toward them by another child. Children are asked to count, 1, 2, 3, etc., when the ball contacts their hands. Two children may play, pushing the ball back and forth, counting simply 1, 2, 1, 2, . . . , or counting progressively from 1 to 10. A circle of children may also play the game, letting the ball go around the periphery or pushing the ball back and forth across the circle, while counting in a progressive way as the ball contacts "your" hands.

Modifications: Some children can give problems, and others can answer them by pushing the ball the number of times that represents a problem, or a problem component, or an answer. For example, a child can call out 2 + 2, and the other children, using the ball, can push it back and forth the required four times.

GAME 41   Counting: My Friends and Things

Equipment: Beans, stones, other units that can be counted.

Method: Children are asked to gather in groups. They are then asked to count the number in the group. Care must be taken to count themselves. The group members are asked to check the count taken by the first, by also making the count. Next the first child is asked to count marbles, stones, or beans (etc.), and place the same number in a pile, corresponding to the number in his group.

Modifications: If the group is sufficiently advanced, they can be asked to inscribe the corresponding Arabic number on a blackboard. The groups, or sets of objects, can be gradually added to, either separately or in concert: that is, as a person is added to the group, a corresponding object may be added to a pile. The reverse process can also take place—a person may step from the group, while a corresponding object may be taken from the pile of objects. Addition of members as well as subtraction of members may be done with vigor; for instance running, skipping, and the like.

GAME 42   Children in Sets, They May Come and Go

Equipment: A large area, blackboard, objects that may be grouped (for instance, balls, beans, rocks etc.).

Method: Groups of children are formed, sizes of from two to four are best at first. Next, the groups count members to determine numbers in each group. Checks are made by all group members next, and then objects are formed in similar size groups next to each "people group." Finally, simple addition and subtraction may be introduced, as first one child and then more either are added to or leave a group. After an addition (of one or more) has occurred, children should re-count their group; after a child (or children) have left, a similar count should be made. Corresponding additions and subtractions should be made in groups of objects.

Modifications: Introductory multiplication can be introduced, as two groups of three are combined, for example. As a larger group is divided, introduction to division can take place. Children can work first with objects in groups, subtracting and adding, or multiplying and dividing, and then transfer to people-groups may take place. The reverse may also take place, using people-groups first, and then transferring to object groups.

GAME 43   What Do Numbers Look Like?
What Shall I Call Them?

Equipment: Movable numbers (0 through 9) on cards approximately 8 in. × 8 in. in size, blackboard, and objects that may be grouped and counted.

Method: This game requires that children match single numbers, one at a time. A number is written on the board, and a single number, on a card, is placed in front of the child on the floor. If the numbers match, the child jumps on the number in front of her; if not, the game continues. In this way the child is gradually introduced to numbers, one at a time, instead of trying to discriminate between all ten numbers at once, as is necessary in the games that follow. The child may pick up the card in front of her and place it next to the letter on the board, to check the match. Asymmetrical numbers (excluding 0, 1, and 8) are identified also by having the child place her left or right hand on the board, identifying the asymmetry verbally, saying, for example, "The tall part of the 4 is toward my right side," or perhaps, "the 3 opens to my left."

Modifications: Number-identification competition may be encouraged using teams, with one team "up" while the other records correct and incorrect responses. After three mistakes (outs) the teams change roles and the members of the up team become judges, while the judging team is presented with numbers to match one at a time. Several pairs of judges and responders can employ an entire large class. Checks on accuracy can take place, using object or people groups as seen in Games 41 and 42.

GAME 44   Look and Match

Equipment: Number squares, blackboard.

Method: Two squares are placed on the ground in front of a child or two children. A number is written on the board, and the child (or children) must jump into the appropriate matching number in front of him.

Modifications: Increase the number of numbers from which to choose; write a number and then erase it and allow increasingly long periods of time to elapse before permitting movement response to correct larger square (for example, jumping).

GAME 45   Hear, Say, and Jump

Equipment: Number squares, blackboard.

1	5	4	3	5	7	0
6	0	2	7	8	9	8
9	5	6	4	3	1	3
4	2	4	2	6	3	2
1	8	5	7	0	9	1

Method: Teacher or student teacher says a number, and child must find it on the grid containing numbers and jump into the appropriate matching number.

Modifications: More than one number can be called at a time, and child must find two, three, four or more numbers in this manner. An increasing number of choices can be placed in front of the child. A time lapse can be introduced between hearing the number(s) and the movement response produced by the child or children.

GAME 46   Drawing, Touching, and Jumping

Equipment: Cardboard, scissors, squares containing numbers.

Method: Numbers can be cut out, written on board, talked about, touched, and then found and jumped in on the grid.

Modifications: Children may need to spend a day or a week on a single number in this manner. Children can hold up a cut-out number and then ask a partner to find it on the square and jump into it. Numbers can be written in various sizes, can be cut out in various sizes, and then jumped into or hopped into in various ways on the grids.

GAME 47   Run Through It

Equipment: Lined figures, made using lining tape, painted lines, or grooves in a large sandbox; blackboard.

Method: Number is either called out verbally or written on board. Child must then find it by running through its shape within the more complex patterns. Increasing difficulty can be elicited if the child must run her own pattern without any guides (for instance, on an unmarked grass or cement area or when more than one number at a time is called and then more than one is "traced" via running movements). Children can also jump, hop, skip, move backward, or otherwise negotiate the appropriate pattern.

Modifications: Child can first write number on a card and then, holding it, try to run through appropriate pattern. Number can be erased prior to jumping in it or hopping in it.

GAME 48   More Numbers, Many Digits

Equipment: Blackboard, number squares.

Method: Two-digit or three-digit numbers are written on blackboard. Child must jump into both digits or place one foot in one and the second in the other. If three- or four- or more-digit numbers are used, child may either jump into each in order or place a hand, foot, and foot in the three if possible.

Modifications: Numbers may be given verbally and then found in the above manner. One child may find two or three numbers in order on the jumping grids and then, observing another child or children, say which numbers they are (for example, 10, 131, etc.).

GAME 49   Running in the Sand

Equipment: Blackboard, sandbox.

Method: Child must run through a number's shape in the sandbox after first hearing it or seeing it written on the blackboard.

Modifications: Races of this nature can take place using two or more children at the same time or at different times. Numbers can be first run through and then written on the board; written numbers can be erased and then increasingly long periods of time be allowed to elapse before permitting children to run through them in the sand. The child can hold a series of cards in his hand, containing all numbers, and at the same time try to run through each one in order, shuffling to the top of the pile the card containing the number dealt with.

GAME 50   Spaceship

Equipment: Blackboard, a spaceship as shown done with a painted line or with lining tape.

| 10 | 9 | 8 | 7 | 6 | 5 | 4 | 3 | 2 | 1 |

Method: Practice jumping along the numbers and counting while executing the countdown and blasting off the spaceship. Observing children can check accuracy.

Modifications: Handicapped children can throw balls or bean bags in order in each square, calling out appropriate number as they land in each one. Numbers can be done in any order. Number can be written on board and then found on the spaceship or vice versa. When a number is jumped in and named correctly, the child can then write it on the board.

A more concrete idea of quantity may be exhibited by having the children place individual units (beans, rocks, beads etc.) of the correct number in the correct numbered square. Thus, next to, or in the square containing the numeral 5, five objects may be placed.

GAME 51 Counting Relays

Equipment: Two or more sets of number squares, blackboard.

Method: One member at a time from each of two teams runs to a location, finds a number (starting with 1), returns to her team with the number, places it on the ground, and tags the next team member, who returns to same location and obtains the second number in order (that is, 2), and then repeats process. Winning team finishes first. More than nine members on a team may be used if numbering is either started over again after reaching 9 or if two squares are obtained.

Modifications: Children may be asked to jump, hop, or skip for numbers. Two children at a time from each team may go for a single number, each holding it when returning on the run. The number may be obtained in random order, triggered by series of numbers on the blackboard (i.e., 6859321).

GAME 52   Run and Jump: Counting Relays

Equipment: Two or more grids containing all numbers in individual squares.

Method: One member at a time from each of two teams runs to grid and jumps into appropriate squares (i.e., first 1, then 2, etc.). Then he returns to his team, tags the next child, etc., until all numbers are used. Two-digit numbers may also be used (tenth child must jump into 1 and 0 squares, eleventh into 1 and 1 squares, etc.). Counting backward can also be used (100 through 1).

Modifications: Numbers, either one- or two-digit, may be thrown into or jumped into by the teams in random order with the numbers placed on a blackboard in front of the teams. Numbers can be alternated (that is, 1 on board, 2 jumped into, 3 written, 4 jumped into, etc.).

GAME 53   Jump and Count

Equipment: Grid containing number squares.

Method: One or more children, using one or several grids, jump from 1 to any other number in order. They may count to any number in this manner, using two- and then three-digit numbers. Count out loud as number is landed in; observing children check accuracy.

Modifications: Speed races may be held against each other or against a clock (for instance, "How fast can you count to 50 by jumping in the appropriate squares in the right order?").

GAME 54   See Quick and Hop

Equipment: Flash cards containing numbers, number squares.

Method: Number is flashed briefly, and child must make response into appropriate matching square on the grid (for example, hop into it).

Modifications: A time lapse may be introduced after the flash card is seen. The flash can be accompanied by verbal identification of the number by child and/or by teacher.

GAME 55   Partner Write and Tell

Equipment: Blackboard(s), grids containing large number squares.

Method: Children work in partners. One jumps and the other writes a number on the board. Child may first jump and then write, or the writing child can cue the jumping child as to what to do. Competing teams can see who can finish a series of numbers first (that is, numbers written on card for team member using blackboard).

Modifications: Writing partner can both write and say number, or she can be required to write number and then erase it prior to asking partner to jump into square. She can write one number and then make the game work by adding a given number to it each time (for example, write 2, but must add 3 before jumping response, 5).

GAME 56   How Many Can You?

Equipment: Number squares.

Method: Each child has his own number square and must execute three, four, or five things into or around each square. He chooses his own things (for instance, jump into it, jump on it forward, hop over it, run around it). There are thousands of possibilities. An observing child counts the responses of the moving child, and then the roles are reversed.

Modifications: The size of the number may signal the number of things required (for example, the 3 square means you must do three things to it). Children may move from smaller to larger numbers in this manner. Children should be given time to think of their own things in this game.

GAME 57   How Many Did I?

Equipment: Number squares.

Method: Similar to Game 55, but children compete in teams of two or more to see how many different things they can do to their numbers. The team or individual thinking of the most original things is the winner. Observing children judge originality.

Modifications: You might limit what they may do to specific categories (for instance, one-legged things, blackboard things, jumping things, going around things).

GAME 58   How Far Can You Jump?

Equipment: Twenty lines, about 3 in. long, placed 2 in. apart. They are made with tape or paint on a mat, floor, or cement surface.

Method: After a standing broadjump is executed, children determine how far they went by counting lines they traversed. Competition can be introduced; backward broadjumping can be a modification; sideways jumping for distance can also be used. Actual distance can be computed by multiplying lines by 2.

Modifications: Child can experiment with various arm movements while jumping (for example, leaving them down at sides, throwing them upward or forward and upward). Self-estimation of future success can take place prior to first jump and before successive attempts. Measurement between estimations and actual performance may be most revealing. Ball thrown for distance can be done in a similar manner, using a long tape measure.

GAME 59   Find the Sign

Equipment: Number squares containing numbers and arithmetical signs ($=$, $+$, $-$, $\div$, $\times$).

Method: Using the squares, children are first verbally told the name of a sign and they must then find it by jumping into it on the grid. Discussion should continue to define the operation or operations indicated by the sign.

Modifications: Advanced children can continue on and jump simple addition and subtraction problems (for instance, $2 + 2 = 4$) by hopping in the appropriate squares. Or, they can act out operations by using blank squares and carrying them apart and together when adding or subtracting operations are discussed. The grid may also be expanded to include pictures, for example, pictures of animals. Thus, by jumping, a child may pose a rather concrete problem to other children, such as 4 rabbits plus 6 rabbits equals __? Additional squares may be added to include xs and ys, thus permitting problems in algebra to be "asked" by one child of another. For instance, $7 = x + 4$ may be used in this context, and the child answering must then jump a $x = 3$.

GAME 60   Collect and Count

Equipment: Letter squares or blank squares.

Method: Children run to a central pile of squares, gather two or more, return and collect more, and count each group they collect. Each time they return with their squares, they count the number they have added together.

Modifications: Other children, by jumping in appropriate squares, may cue the running children as to how many squares to bring back. They then can jump the answer to the simple addition problem as the other children are counting the squares to obtain the answer.

GAME 61   Take Away the Squares

Equipment: Squares, either blank or containing numbers and letters.

Method: Children start with a pile of five or six squares and then take away one or more squares, counting first the initial number and then the final number.

Modifications: Children can cue one another concerning the original number, how many to take away, and the expected answer, by jumping into the appropriate numbers on a letter grid containing larger squares.

GAME 62 Jump the Answer

Equipment: Blackboard and squares containing numbers and signs.

Method: A simple problem in addition or subtraction is placed on the board, and children try to jump into number squares indicating the correct answer. Two-digit answers can be indicated by separate movements or by placing each foot in a separate square.

Modifications: Children can give problems verbally to one another or can write them on the board. Problems of increased complexity can be offered in this manner. Competition for speed of correct answers can be introduced between two or more children. Observing children can verify correctness of answers of jumping or hopping children.

GAME 63 Hop the Problems

Equipment: Blackboard, grid containing number squares.

Method: Child jumps a problem using number grids containing appropriate signs (plus and minus). Observing child, at another grid or at a blackboard, indicates the answer (by writing or by jumping into appropriate squares). Thus a problem is jumped out in concrete terms $(2 + 2 = \_)$.

Modifications: Children can attempt to first write and then duplicate a problem by jumping in squares. Subtraction and addition can be made even more concrete by having squares contain pictures of rabbits, etc., so that the child can be jumping 2 rabbits + 4 rabbits = 6 rabbits. Observing children can check correctness of problems and responses.

GAME 64   Jump and Reach

Equipment: Twenty lines placed 1 or 2 in. apart on the vertical surface of a gymnasium wall or on a classroom wall.

Method: Start with the shortest child in the class. The child first stands against the wall, with both toes against it, and reaches upward, arms straight, to see how high she can reach. She then turns to the side and tries to jump and touch as far above her standing-plus-reach height as she can. Score is computed by subtracting standing reach from jumping reach.

Modifications: Children may experiment with jumping mechanics to determine, for example, whether or not lifting the arms adds significantly to the jumping height. Children may compute efficiency by comparing ratios of heights to the amount over height jumped by individual class members. Maximum leg girth (circumference of thigh at largest point) may be contrasted (correlated) to jumping height, minus standing height. Boys and girls in various competitive sports may be compared and contrasted.

GAME 65   Addition Relays

Equipment: Grids containing squares with numbers and mathematical signs.

Method: One member at a time from each of two teams jumps out a problem in his grid. The second member from each team jumps out the answer. A checker from the opposite team determines the accuracy of the response. This procedure continues, problem alternated with answer, until all members of the team are finished and the winning team is determined by speed and accuracy. Inaccurate answers must be rejumped by the child after being corrected.

Modifications: Team members may have to run, hop, or in some other way move a distance to the grid prior to executing the problem and answer.

GAME 66 Subtraction Runs

Equipment: Blackboard, grids containing numbers (one for each team).

Method: Both teams start with 100 points. A member from each team runs to his grid and jumps into a one-digit number, which is subtracted by another team member on the blackboard from 100. The next team members run and jump into a second number, which is subtracted from this first remainder. This procedure continues until all team members compete one or more times. Accuracy is checked on by observers. The last child running becomes the subtractor at the blackboard and then returns to the end of the line.

Modifications: Teams may work in pairs, one observing and the other jumping. Teams may start with 1,000 or more points and jump two-digit numbers before subtracting them each time.

GAME 67 Take-Away Broadjumps

Equipment: Twenty 3-in. lines placed 1 or 2 in. apart on a horizontal surface (the floor of a gymnasium, a classroom, a cement surface, or a mat; see illustration on page 84).

Method: Children, one at a time, execute a standing broadjump to see how far they can travel. They use the lines to land on and measure their jumps. Next, starting from the same point, they execute a backward broadjump. Subtract the two scores to find the difference.

Modifications: To find out the effects of learning, they may also subtract their first attempt at either forward or backward broadjumping from the final attempt.

GAME 68   Throwing Best Subtraction

Equipment: Tape measure 100 to 150 ft. long, balls of various kinds and sizes.

Method: Children should be permitted to throw along the length of the tape to see how far they can throw using various techniques (that is, underhand, using a run into the throw, overhand, using a step into the throw) and various different sizes of balls. Subtraction problems can then be computed on a blackboard to compare the distances thrown with various kinds of balls.

Modifications: Throwing contests can be run. Children can look at learning improvement using various techniques, comparing first attempts to subsequent efforts.

GAME 69   Decimal Races

Equipment: Stopwatches, running surface 30 to 100 yd. long, score cards, clipboards.

Method: Take team scores in running a given distance, by addition of tenths of seconds, of all members' efforts (low score wins).

Modifications: Course can be circular. Distances can vary for various group members with different capabilities. Each member can get three or more trials and her best trial computed for the team effort. Children can hop, skip, or otherwise negotiate the course.

GAME 70   Team Base Count and Add

Equipment: Diamond with three or four bases, playground ball, blackboard or numbers in grid.

Method: The team up hits, one at a time, sending the ball to the outfield. The team in the field retrieves the ball, lines up with the retriever in the front of line, and passes the ball quickly to the rearmost member, who yells "Stop." The hitter circles as many bases as possible before "Stop" is called, continuing past home if he is able and making additional circuits of the bases. A progressive score is kept on the blackboard of all team members' efforts. Then the fielding team goes to bat.

Modifications: Score can also be kept on grid, or child on grid can jump into squares corresponding to bases passed by runner. Children can hop, skip, or do something other than run bases.

GAME 71   Multiplying and Dividing My Classmates

Equipment: Blackboard, objects (balls, beans, marbles, etc.), groups of from four to forty children.

Method: Using groups and set theory, introductions to both multiplication and division may be made by using the children themselves as units in groups. Children may be placed in a group of twelve "eggs"—"now you are a dozen eggs. Now divide into two equal groups ... count how many are now in each group of a half-dozen eggs. ... Now get into three equal size groups. How many are there in each group? Now get together again."

This can be continued with variously sized groups and with different number of groups. The operations that take place with the groups may be represented in another concrete manner using objects in sets (for instance, piles of beans, etc.). On a more abstract level, if the children are ready, the processes may be depicted on the blackboard, using Arabic numbers and the appropriate symbols ($\times$ and $\div$).

Modifications: Transfer to blackboard representation may occur in either of two ways—by moving from people arrangements to the board or by first starting with a multiplication or division problem presented on the board and then moving to a problem using people and objects. Using hand calculators, evaluators can check the accuracy of the operations carried out.

Children who are beginning to conceptualize about addition and subtraction may be taken one step farther. This type of division or multiplication game may be conducted with children too young for symbolic representation of these processes with Arabic numbers or with children as they begin to use abstract Arabic numbers, in order to make these vague symbols more meaningful.

GAME 72 Time-Tables Leap

Equipment: Blackboard; grids containing number squares; and addition, subtraction, and multiplication signs ($+$, $-$, $\times$).

Method: A multiplication problem is placed on the blackboard. Children singly or in competition with one another try to jump the proper answer. Use one-digit numbers to work on multiplication problems. May be alternated with addition or subtraction problems.

Modifications: Problems can be given via another child jumping into squares in grid. Answer can appear on board or via jumping or hopping again.

GAME 73 Hear and Hop

Equipment: Blackboard, grids containing numbers.

Method: Problems (multiplication, simple addition, or subtraction) are given verbally and then answered via jumping in grid or writing on board.

Modifications: Team competitions can be introduced. A problem can be voiced and time intervals introduced. A child, on getting the right answer, can be permitted to give next problem.

GAME 74   Answer Running

Equipment: Blackboard, patterns made by painted lines or by lining tape as shown here and on page 88.

Method: A variety of mathematics problems can be given verbally or written on the blackboard. Children, in pairs or alone, can attempt to run through the shapes of the answers. Observing children can confirm accuracy. The running child can also voice the answer.

Modifications: A sandbox can be used and the answer run through in sand without any guiding figure. Relays can be played in this manner, using separate grids for each team. Multiplication tables and simple addition and subtraction problems can be answered in this manner.

GAME 75   Progressive Addition

Equipment: Grid containing number squares.

Method: Child jumps from one number to another. An observing child or the jumping child progressively adds the number jumped to the previous total. The observing child then takes the jumper's role.

Modifications: The jumping child can compete with the observing child to see which can reach a total first at each jump and then an overall total after ten or more jumps. A child at the blackboard, writing the same numbers, can compete with the observing child and with the jumping child to see who can add most accurately and quickly. Parallels between progressive addition and multiplication can be depicted in additional games or explained as this game is played.

GAME 76   Problems and Answers

Equipment: Blackboard, at least two grids containing squares with numbers and operations signs ($-$, $\times$, $+$, $=$, $\div$).

Method: A child on one grid jumps out a problem, and a child on the second grid jumps the answer. Then they reverse roles. This procedure alternates with observing children checking accuracy. An inaccurate answer can change a jumper to an observer.

Modifications: Other children can observe and record answers on blackboards adjacent to grids. Children can remain in one operation (for example, multiplication tables) or can constantly change operations. The addition of pictures to the grid may make multiplication and division more meaningful, as a child jumps problems ("5 cows, times 6 cows, equals _____?").

GAME 77   Percentage Basketball

Equipment: TV set, basketball game, clipboards, score cards.

Method: Records of basketball players' shots are taken. Shots made from the field or the free-throw line can be collected and percentages of success computed (that is, dividing total shots taken into number made). An actual game or a TV game can be scored.

Modifications: Team percentages of each type of shot can be recorded. Shot charts can indicate from where on court shots are taken and percentages of shots successful at various distances from the basket. Compare the percentages of losing to winning teams.

GAME 78   Track Division

Equipment: Two stopwatches, track meet (televised or visited), clipboards, score cards.

Method: Clock the total relay time and divide by the number of legs run. Compare with actual clockings of these legs. Compare the total time of longer races (one-half mile and over) with number obtained, dividing total time by number of laps. Compare to actual lap times, clocked to the nearest tenth of a second. Compare winning times to second- and third-place times in various races. Compute percentage differences and actual differences.

Modifications: Use bar graphs to compare lap times of individuals, of relay racers, and of first-, second-, and third-place finishers.

GAME 79 Finding Out About Football

Equipment: Clipboards, score cards, football game (actual or televised).

Method: Compute yardage gained by two teams (passing versus running). Divide by the number of plays run to see the yards per play of each type. Compute the same data for individual players. Each observing child may have a different player to score. Compute the yardage gained by pass catchers, after catching passes, and because of distance pass travels. Compute kicking distances and average per kick.

Modifications: Graph the results, comparing critical differences in losing versus winning team. Score the times each team lost the ball. Compare statistics obtained by quarter; compare these data to the scores by quarters.

SUMMARY AND OVERVIEW

A wide variety of arithmetic operations and concepts are contained in the games presented within this chapter. The teacher may employ these in numerous ways to enrich and enhance mathematics lessons at both the primary and secondary school levels. Most important, the activities present opportunities to make quantity a more concrete idea than it often is to children attempting to deal with abstract Arabic numerals. Many of the games require children to use either their own bodies or other objects as units, and thus to represent quantitative ideas in clear and concrete ways.

BIBLIOGRAPHY

BRUSH, L.R. Preschool children's knowledge of addition and subtraction. *Journal for Research in Mathematics Education*, 1978, *9*, 49-59.

GINSBURG, H.P. *Children's arithmetic: The learning process.* New York: Van Nostrand, 1977.

GROEN, G.J., and RESNICK, L.B. Can preschool children invent addition algorithms? *Journal of Educational Psychology*, 1977, *69*, 645-652.

HAMRICK, K.B. Oral language and readiness for the written symbolization of addition and subtraction. *Journal for Research in Mathematics Education*, 1979, *10*, 188-194.

HENDRICKSON, A.D. An inventory of mathematical thinking done by incoming first-grade children. *Journal for Research in Mathematics Education*, 1979 *10*, 7-23.

HUMPHREY, J. *A comparison of the use of the physical education learning medium with traditional procedures in the development of certain arithmetical processes in second grade children.* Unpublished paper, Univ. of Maryland, 1968.

————. An exploratory study of active games in learning of number concepts by first-grade boys and girls. *Perceptual and Motor Skills*, 1966, *23*, 1011-1013.

OWEN, C. A motoric approach to teaching multiplication to the mentally retarded child. *Education and Training of the Mentally Retarded*, 1976, *1*, 129-134.

PIAGET, J. *The child's conception of number.* New York: Norton, 1952.

ROSS, D. Incidental learning of number concepts in small group games. *American Journal of Mental Deficiency*, 1970, *54*, 718-725.

SIMON, H.A. *The sciences of the artificial.* Cambridge, MA: M.I.T. Press, 1969.

WANG, M.C., RESNICK, L.B., and BOOZER, R.F. The sequence of development of some early mathematics behaviors. *Child Development*, 1971, *42*, 1767-1778.

CHAPTER 6

Letters, Spelling, and Reading

The confrontation with the words and letters of one's native tongue generally begins in the fifth or sixth year in the United States. In other countries, children often enter school a year or two later. The process of learning to read involves a great deal of work for a child. The games in this chapter deal with only a few of the many operations and concepts necessary to this process. Thus these games should be understood to represent only a few of the cobblestones needed to make up the whole "medieval square" of the language arts curriculum.

Many theories and models have attempted to explain the manner in which normal children acquire spoken and written language. Early ideas about the complex processes and subprocesses involved seemed to indicate that the learning of each rule and each word required a specific effort. More modern theories indicate, however, that a child's acquisition of reading and language skills consists of first gaining an awareness of the basic rules that govern word construction, letter-sound combination, and similar perceptual and conceptual combinations and operations, and then generalizing from those rules (Chomsky 1980; Marchanks and Levin 1965).

Essentially, the child must first realize that letters, and the shapes they make when combined in pairs and into words, have meanings and sounds. The recognition of letters involves a new sense of orientation in space. Prior to beginning school, children are familiar only with objects that could be named "correctly" regardless of their precise spatial orientation. A spoon was a spoon, whether lying on the floor or on a table. In school, the youngster is confronted with a rather rigid and new set of orientation rules by his first teacher, who refuses to give to approval to Es, Fs, and Gs that face in the "wrong" direction (Watt and Jacobs 1975).

Lists of the skills necessary to reading abound in the literature. However, most who work on the understanding that reading is a cognitive act postulate that the following processes are the most important underpinnings of reading and of understanding what is read. Experts do not always agree, however, in what order these skills must be acquired. These processes include:

1. The child must be able to speak and to understand the language spoken to him or her in a reasonable fashion.

2. The child should become able to dissect spoken words into component sounds. This is sometimes called acquiring "word attack" skills.

3. The child must learn to recognize and to discriminate between the various letter forms to which he or she is exposed. These include upper and lower case letters, script and printing, and so on. (Cratty 1981).

4. The child must learn the right-left principles that govern the orientation of letters, the arrangement of letters in words, and the direction one reads across a page.

5. The child must learn which sounds are probable outcomes of which letter combinations.

6. The child must learn to recognize printed words by referring to a number of cues. These cues include their general shape, the first letter and the letters that follow, and the sounds the letters evoke. Words must be recognized by the context in which they appear.

7. The child must be able to translate spoken words and phrases to written words and phrases, and vice versa.

8. The child must learn to read, and to think about what is read, to the limits of his or her intellectual capacity.

It is possible to translate all these processes into movement experiences. However, it is not always necessary to do so. Indeed at times acting out concepts and operations of this nature is time-consuming and cumbersome. At the same time it has been found in numerous studies that the use of active experiences may enhance learning of language, reading, spelling, and letter recognition in both typical and atypical groups of children and youth (Cratty and Martin 1971; Hendrickson and Muehl 1962; Jeffrey 1958; Thornburg and Fisher 1970; Humphrey 1967; Asher 1965; Van Osdol, Johnson, and Geiger 1974).

Early in our own research, working with slow learning children in schools in the center of Los Angeles, we found that various conditions were necessary to optimize the use of active academic games within an educational setting. For example, it was apparent that simple letter-recognition games were not as useful as games that combined letter recognition with letter-sound relationships. We discovered that when various serial-memory tasks were combined with phonics games, improvement in spelling lists that had not been specifically practiced, was apparent (Cratty and Martin 1971).

Van Osdol, Johnson, and Geiger (1974) elaborated upon our work with phonics games, using a grid containing various vowel sounds.

The research we carried out involved two- to-three-time-a-week practice of these games within the regular school setting. Children who had been labelled 'slow learners' were able to benefit from working at these activities in groups of six, seven, or eight more than were those placed within passive tutoring situations, in groups of the same size. Additionally these activities worked best when combined with the sort of self-control activities presented in Chapter 2.

The effectiveness of the activities that follow depends upon their judicious use and their appropriate combination with similar activities taking place in the classroom setting. Moreover, all these games are not appropriate all the time for all children. The efficiency depends upon just how they are employed in order to match the language-arts needs of both special children and those who simply enjoy enriching and motivating activities of this kind.

The presentations of many of the games include discussions of how a child's auditory or visual memory may be enhanced. For example, in some of the activities a time delay is introduced between the time a letter is presented and the time at which a child is expected to respond. It is believed that the type of subvocal rehearsal that will usually be engaged in, and the process of visual imagery that will be evoked during this time period are helpful perceptual-cognitive exercises.

Also, as in other games in the book, modifications may be made to accommodate handicapped children. Children confined to wheelchairs enjoy throwing bean bags or other missiles in order to participate in the tasks outlined.

GAME 80   Up Letters and Down Letters

Equipment: Ropes, balls, blackboard, floor space or mat space.

Method: In order to help children begin to distinguish between up and down when viewing space, various pairs of up and down symbols may be used on the board, such as:

A movement is associated with each symbol. The child is then asked to distinguish between the two symbols by performing the appropriate movement when each is displayed. From symbols the game may progress to up and down letters—letters that in order to be correct must be written in an up-down orientation. These include *U, T, I, M, W, A,* and the like. A movement response is now required for presentation of a correctly oriented up-down letter. Thus a correct *U* might be represented by a jump, while an incorrectly oriented ∩ should not be responded to.

The balls, ropes, etc., may be used in several ways within this game. For example, a child may, if the proper symbol appears, jump over or crawl under a rope. Likewise, a physical response with the ball may involve throwing the ball up or throwing it down in response to an up or down symbol.

Modifications: Up-down in vertical space (on the blackboard) is toward-away on a desk top or on any horizontal surface. This kind of transfer should be taught specifically. This game may also be used as part of phonics practice, with the child required to give a movement response as well as the correct sound (or a word containing the sound) when an up or down letter is presented.

GAME 81   Left Letters and Right Letters

Equipment: Ropes, balls, blackboard, floor space, and/or mat space.

Method: The point of this game is to aid children in discriminating between letters that "face" right or left. They are first confronted with pairs of asymmetrical symbols that have either a right or left orientation. These kinds of asymmetrical symbols might include:

Different movement responses are associated with each of the symbols in the pair, and when each symbol is written on the board the child must make the "correct" response. Next asymmetrical letters are presented, including *D, d, E, r, C, S, s, Q, J, K,* and the like, and a movement response is required for presentation of a correctly oriented letter. Thus a correct *E* might be represented by a jump, while an incorrectly oriented E should not be responded to.

Left letters, or right letters, when they appear, may be responded to by throwing a ball to the appropriate direction, or to a classmate in either direction from the thrower. Ropes placed to either side of the child may be jumped over, either moving to the left or right, when a letter opening that is closed on that side appears. For instance, an open C may mean jump to the right, or throw a ball to the right, while a J whose curve is to the left when presented correctly, may require a response to the child's left, either by jumping over a rope to the left, or throwing a ball to the same direction.

Modifications: Youngsters may also be confronted with correct and incorrect orientations of words (for instance, *as* vs. *sa*), and asked to make a movement response when word is correctly presented. Asymmetrical letters may be sounded out, or both acted upon and sounded.

GAME 82   Slants in Letters

Equipment: Blackboard, ropes, balls, floor space, and/or mat space.

Method: Slanted lines are presented in pairs, with the child required to make a different movement response to each. By observing the correctness of the movement response, the teacher may determine whether the child can recognize slanted lines that go from upper left to lower right and the reverse. These slanted stimuli, to which this first part of the game (a coding game) might be as follows: Children may be asked to place a rope so that it slants in the same direction as the middle part of the N, or perhaps to let a ball fall like the vertical line in a letter presented.

Next, various "slanted" letters are presented, including Z, R, K, R, N, as well as lower case letters such as z, r, and the like, and a movement response is required for those in correct orientation. Thus presentation of a correctly written N might require a jump in response, while an incorrect Ͷ might require that the child stand motionless.

Modifications: This game may also include practice in sounding out the letters or in forming a word with the letter sound in it. The game may also be combined with other letter orientation coding games, with a four or five element symbol-to-movement code learned to curved, slanted, asymmetrical, and symmetrical up-down letters. A letter when shown, for example, may need to be sounded out, and then an action verb having that sound may have to be executed. A sound may be given by the teacher, at which point the child must both write the correct letter, and, using the rope and perhaps a ball (to dot the *i*?), must replicate that letter on the playground. A rope may be then used to play a game within the letter shape it has formed.

GAME 83   Letter Build-Up

Equipment: Single letter squares containing upper- or lower-case letters, blackboard.

Method: A single lettered square is placed on the ground in front of a child, and then the same or a different letter is written on the board. If the letters match, the child makes a physical response (for instance, jumping) into the lettered square; if not, she makes no response. It is best to start with hard consonants, such as *t* and *d*. The game gradually builds up the number of discriminations the child must make. At first the child simply has to decide whether a letter is an *A* or not an *A*. Next two letter squares are placed in front of the child, a single letter is written on the board, and the child must decide whether to respond at all and, if so, which square to move into. Then three letter squares are placed before the child, and so on. This game should come before those in which a grid containing twenty-six or more letters is used, as in the games that follow.

Modifications: The child may be given a sound and then asked to respond in the manner described above to one or more letters or letter combinations on squares placed in front of her. Alternatively, the child may be given a single letter and asked to respond with the correct sound or with a word that includes that sound. Children just learning letters and their sounds, and handicapped children, may make modified movement responses to letters in front of them that match letters printed on the blackboard.

GAME 84   Match and Jump

Equipment: Blackboard, letter squares, chalk.

Method: Child observes block letter printed on board and from two choices attempts to indicate correct match by jumping in the appropriate letter square. The board is erased, another letter is written, and a choice is made from two or three squares.

Modifications: Increase the number of squares to from three up to twenty-six. Vary the response requested (for example, hop, jump around, run around). The handicapped child may throw a bean bag into the squares of his choice. Another child may act as teacher, writing a letter or number on the board, while a third child may observe and correct the jumper. The game becomes more difficult if the letter is written and then erased prior to eliciting a response from the child.

GAME 85   Tell, Find, and Tell

Equipment: Letter and number squares.

Method: The child is told a letter verbally. She must then find it from two or more choices, jump in it, and at the same time repeat verbally the name of the letter. More than one letter at a time can be called prior to eliciting more than one jump.

Modifications: The child must choose from among an increasing number of choices. Increase the period of time allowed to elapse between telling by teacher (or another child) and the responses made by the learner (jumping and telling again). A chain-reaction game may be played as a child jumps and tells after being told and then in turn jumps and tells on another letter, which must be repeated by a third child, then a fourth child, etc.

GAME 86   Find Them

Equipment: Blackboard, lined patterns using painted lines or lining tape as shown.

Method: Letters are placed on the blackboard, one at a time. Students are required to find them in the complex patterns and confirm them by running through the shapes.

Modifications: Students may first write them again. Before running, they may hop or skip through patterns. Observing students can check on accuracy. Running through a letter or number may precede writing it on the board.

GAME 87   The Sandbox

Equipment: Sandbox, blackboard.

Method: Write a letter (or tell it), and then ask the child to walk through its shape in the sandbox. An observing child can correct errors. The walking child can see his own footprints. He must wipe the sand level after walking to ensure inspection of subsequent footprints.

Modifications: The teacher may start with simple geometric patterns and gradually progress to letter shapes. The child may first inspect numbers and letters in a horizontal plane before walking them in the same plane. The transposition from a vertical plane (blackboard) to a horizontal plane (sandbox) can cause problems.

GAME 88   Playground Letters

Equipment: Blackboard or clipboards containing paper, playground (unmarked).

Method: After showing a child a simple geometric figure or letter shape, ask him to run or walk through its shape on the playground. Ask an observing child to check accuracy. (Note: Footprints will not leave marks as in Game 87.)

Modifications: A child may be asked to run through a series of letters or a whole sentence. This type of task is an extremely difficult undertaking.

GAME 89   Alphabet Games

Equipment: Letter squares.

Method: Children, one at a time, may select in correct order, the letters of the alphabet. The letters may then be arranged in order and talked about as the children hop or jump on them.

Modifications: Letters may be lower-case or upper-case. They may be jumped on backward or forward, from the A or from the Z in the alphabet. Relays may be run to see which team can construct a line of letter squares forming the alphabet first. A teacher or student "caller" can call the correct letters in order, to which responding children can react by selecting appropriate letter squares and arranging them in the proper order.

GAME 90   Letter Hopscotch

Equipment: Blackboard, letter squares arranged in grid and placed together as shown.

G	F	U	B	V	K
O	Y	N	S	D	L
U	A	I	Q	E	O
T	Y	Z		R	X
D	W	M	C	B	I
P	J	E	A	H	S

Method: One or more children can attempt to respond quickly to letters, written one at a time on the board or given orally one at a time, by jumping into the corresponding square on the grid as shown.

Modifications: Children can hop, compete with one another, or work alone. Children can call letters aloud to themselves as they jump from letter to letter in a single row (thus six children can work at a time). After jumping in correct letter, given orally, the child can be asked to copy it on the board. Letter locations should be changed frequently to avoid recognition by location rather than shape.

GAME 91   Letter Relays

Equipment: Blackboard, score sheets, squares containing letters.

Method: One child at a time from each of two teams should be asked to go to a group of letters, run back with one, place it in order, and tag the next member of her team. Repeat until the entire series of letters (the alphabet) is placed side by side. The winning team is the one that completes the series first.

Modifications: Children in wheelchairs can be wheeled for letters. Normal children can be encouraged to use a variety of movement patterns, such as hopping, skipping, etc.

GAME 92   Cutting, Looking, and Finding

Equipment: Paper, scissors, letter squares, blackboard.

Method: Have the child cut out a letter, find it on the letter grid, jump in it, and draw it on the blackboard. The child then cuts out two or more letters, holds them in his hand while he jumps into their corresponding letter on the grid, and shuffles a new letter to the top of the pack after each jump.

Modifications: For some groups of children a single letter may be a project for a single day (or week). They must find out all about the letter in all its forms by cutting, touching, drawing, looking, and finding it on the grids.

GAME 93   Flash and Jump

Equipment: Flash cards containing numbers, letter squares to jump in.

Method: Letters are flashed briefly, one at a time. The child must then recognize the letter and jump in the appropriate letter match on the larger squares.

Modifications: Two children may compete, first observing the flash card and then attempting to jump first into the appropriate matching squares. Both upper-case and lower-case letters may be used (that is, flash lower-case and jump in upper-case letters). Handicapped children may throw bean bags into appropriate squares.

GAME 94   Upper-Case, Lower-Case

Equipment: Flash cards, letter squares containing both lower- and upper-case letters in separate squares.

Method: The child may be given a packet of flash cards containing lower-case letters to hold. Observing them one at a time in her hand, she tries to jump in the appropriate upper-case letter on the larger squares. The teacher may flash upper-case letters and have the child attempt, by herself or in competition with another child, to jump in corresponding lower-case letters.

Modifications: A handicapped child may throw bean bags into appropriate squares. Matching may also be done solely in larger squares (that is, a child may first jump into an upper-case letter and then find the corresponding lower-case letter and hop in it). A "student teacher" may show a group of two or three children an upper-case letter by jumping into it, and then the other children can compete to see who can jump first into the corresponding lower-case letter.

GAME 95 Script and Print

Equipment: Blackboard, letter squares containing lower- and upper-case letters.

Method: Letters may be written one at a time on the board in script, and then the child must find the upper-case and lower-case printed equivalent on the appropriate squares by jumping in them, hopping in them, etc.

Modifications: Children may compete in this manner after observing manuscript letters. Increasing periods of time may elapse after a letter is written, and it may be erased prior to permitting a movement response.

GAME 96 Show and Sound

Equipment: Letter squares and blackboard.

Method: Using a blackboard, print hard consonants (*D, B, C, T, K, P,* etc.) and have the child find them on letter grid by jumping in them. Alternatively, have the child using the grid containing hard consonants, jump in each and sound out each hard sound and a word that includes it (for example, jump in *B* and say "*B* as in *boy*," jump in *C* and say "*C* as in *cut*").

Modifications: Teacher or teaching student can say hard consonant sounds, and the child can find the appropriate grid letter and hop in it, jump in it, etc. The handicapped child can throw a bean bag in the appropriate squares.

GAME 97 Sounds of Letters and Letter Combinations

Equipment: Blackboard, matted area or floor space with grid or grids as shown. You may use one or both. Each grid may be modified to correspond to a teacher's method of teaching phonics and may be expanded to include other letters and letter combinations. These grids, like others in this book, may be placed on a wall to be used as targets or on the floor to be thrown or jumped into.

Method: Children are asked to indicate via a physical response what the first, middle, or last sounds are in various words given either visually, orally, or both visually and orally (for instance: "What is the first sound of *indent*?" or "the last sound of *lovely*?" or, perhaps, "the middle sound of *asked*?").

CH	SH	SK
CK	ED	LY

Ĭ	Ŏ
Ý	Ē
Ă	Ŭ
Ō	Y̆
Ū	Á
Ĕ	Ī

Modifications: The physical response may be given first; that is, after throwing or jumping into a given square, a child or children may be asked to form a word whose first, middle, or last sound is composed of the "sound" jumped in. Children learning word attack and phonics skills and children evidencing auditory perception problems and problems matching sounds to letters and letters to sounds may benefit.

GAME 98   Vowel Sounds

Equipment: Letter squares, blackboard.

Method: First make sure the child knows the vowels by name. Then place various vowels on the board, indicating how each should be pronounced by proper accent marks over words (for instance, ä or ā, ē).

The child finds the proper letter in grid squares and confirms her knowledge by jumping or hopping in it.

Modifications: With more advanced children, pronounce a word with the vowel sound and then ask the child to write the vowel sound and to find the vowel by jumping in it, hopping in it, etc.

GAME 99   Consonant Sounds

Equipment: Blackboard, letter squares containing consonants whose sounds are relatively consistent (as shown).

W	J	V	Z
B	M	N	F
V	Y	Z	S
D	F	T	R

Method: The child tells the sound and finds it in the grid by jumping, etc. Conversely, he may jump in the grid and pronounce the sound on arriving there.

Modifications: The child can find sounds within words, make up words having these sounds, and jump them out (correct letters in order, etc.). Handicapped children can "answer" by throwing bean bags, etc.

GAME 100   Spelling: See, Hear, and Spell

Equipment: Blackboard, letter squares (twenty-six letters arranged in grid).

Method: Spell word verbally and write it out on the blackboard. While it remains, the child duplicates the word by jumping in the proper squares in order on the grid.

Modifications: Spell short words verbally only, or write the word but then erase it. The child must duplicate it by jumping or hopping. Two or more children, each with separate grids, attempt to spell letters as quickly as possible in competition. An observing child for each confirms accuracy.

GAME 101   Anagrams

Equipment: Five or more letter squares per child, with each set of five containing at least one vowel.

Method: Each child must jump through as many words as she can with her set of letters. This task becomes increasingly easy as the number of letters allotted each child is increased. Each jumping child should have an observing child counting words and making sure of accurate spelling. Using a grid of thirty-six squares (6 ft. × 6 ft.), six students, each with a row, can play at the same time.

Modifications: Set time limits per set of five words, and then add two letters every two minutes, etc.

GAME 102   Team Spelling

Equipment: Pencils and paper; nine-, sixteen-, twenty-five-, or thirty-six-letter grids.

Method: Divide the children into teams of three or four members each. Each team, using its grid, thinks of as many words as possible. One member records, a second observes spelling, and a third jumps through the word being added to the list. At the end of a time period, lists are compared for number of words and accuracy of spelling.

GAME 103   Spelling Relays

Equipment: Blackboard, letter squares.

Method: Place all letters (several alphabets) together. With two teams of players, place a reasonably long word on the blackboard to spell via a relay. One player from each team runs to get the first letter, returns, and tags a second, who returns with the second, places it next to the first, and in this way spells the entire word. The first team to complete the word wins.

Modifications: For handicapped children, two teams may be formed of children in wheelchairs. One at a time they may be pushed to a letter grid, throw a bean bag with a string attached at the appropriate letter, in order, and then return to have the second child pushed to the grid.

GAME 104   Running Spelling Games

Equipment: Blackboard, lined area containing patterns (as shown) made with lining tape or permanent yellow painted lines.

Method: Using one or two teams, individuals try (against a stopwatch or in competition with one another) to run through all the letters in a given order, using the patterns as shown. The word is placed on the blackboard.

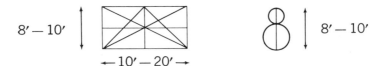

$8' - 10'$ $\longleftarrow 10' - 20' \longrightarrow$ $8' - 10'$

Modifications: The children can use a sandbox, without marked lines. They may skip, hop, or jump through the letters.

GAME 105   Hear and Spell

Equipment: Letter squares.

Method: A word is given aloud, and the child tries to spell it on the grid containing letter squares by jumping, etc., into the appropriate squares.

Modifications: Two children may compete on the same or on different grids to see how fast each can complete the word by jumping or hopping into squares. Words may be spelled by throwing bean bags.

GAME 106   Hearing and Spelling Relays

Equipment: Blackboard, letter squares forming one or more grids.

Method: One member at a time from each of two teams attempts as fast as possible to spell words given orally. The opposite team observes for accuracy. The winning team finishes first after each member has spelled one word.

Modifications: After jumping or hopping out the word, the child may write it on the blackboard. Children in wheelchairs may be pushed one at a time to the grid, into which they may throw bean bags to spell words.

GAME 107   Spell a Story

Equipment: Letter squares.

Method: Two or more children alternately "tell" a story by jumping words in the grid. One child starts with a word; the next child continues the story by a second word, etc., until a story is "told."

Modifications: The story may be a familiar one, but it should be made up by the children. The usual modifications may be made for children who cannot jump or hop.

GAME 108   Same or Opposite

Equipment: Blackboard, letter squares placed in grids or in lines.

Method: A word is spelled on the blackboard, and the child must then jump in the grid a word that has the same or opposite meaning.

Modifications: The first word can be given orally or jumped on the grid, and the second word can be jumped or thrown via bean bags.

GAME 109   Letters Can Mean Things

Equipment: Blackboard, large matted area or floor space, box or chair, a rope, and a hoop.

Method: Children are shown the letter *J* on the blackboard, and told that it means *jump*. The letter is erased and replaced, and children are asked to show (with the correct movement) "what it means." Next an *H* is placed on the board, and children are told it means *hop*. Then *H* is erased and replaced with another *H*, and children are asked to show (by moving) what it means. They are now asked to continue performing either a hop or jump, depending upon whether an *H* or a *J* is shown to them. Next a third letter, a *G*, is shown to them, and they are told it means *go around the chair*. The three letters are then shown alternately, and the children should respond to each. Actions using a ball, rope, or frisbee can be paired also with symbols.

Modifications: These letters can be gradually expanded into entire words. *H* can be expanded into *Hp*, and later into *Hop*. *J* can be changed to *Jmp* and later to *jump*, etc. Also, letters may be overlapped to test the children's ability to analyze and then to combine into a single movement such configurations as Ⴖ (which means hop around the chair), or perhaps Ⴚ (which means go around the chair), etc.

Able preschool children and others being introduced to the concepts of reading should benefit from this game.

GAME 110   Who and Where

Equipment: Blackboard, floor space or matted area, balls, ropes, and the like.

Method: Children are introduced to the concept that letters can stand for action verbs, as in Game 109. This time, the children are given initials corresponding to the first letters of their first names. John becomes *J* and Mary becomes *M*, etc. (Usually working with children in pairs is best.) Next, on the blackboard, either a *J* or an *M* is written before an action verb (or its initial). Next the children are asked to react accordingly. Thus *M H*, (or *M hops*) becomes *Mary hops* and *J J* (or *J jumps*) becomes *John jumps*. Later these first names can be expanded, that is the child may be asked if they will accept that *Jhn* means his name (John) and later if *John* is ok as a representation of his name. Thus the teacher gradually changes the stimuli (the letters and word) while keeping the response the same, and positive transfer will occur.

Next, various locations are indicated by single letters, for instance, *W* for *window* or *C* for *chair*. These letters too may be stretched out to make the complete word. If lower- and upper-case printing are used, after the first initial is used the next letters should be added so as to produce the total word shape; while final letters to be added should not change the shape.

Modifications: Modifications include setting up entire sentences (for example, *Charlie Jumps by the Window*) by starting with the initials as has been described.

GAME 111   Spell It and Do It

Equipment: Letter squares arranged in grid.

Method: The first child spells a verb (for instance, "jump," "skip") by jumping, throwing, hopping, etc., into appropriate squares on the grid. The second child indicates her understanding by performing the action. The second child, if correct, can instruct the first child or a third child in the same manner. Instructions can be a single word ("run") or a phrase ("pick up the pencil").

Modifications: Instructions can be more subtle ("Spell another word for sorry"). Groups of children can perform for one "teacher," who jumps directions.

GAME 112   The Same but Different

Equipment: Blackboard, letter squares.

Method: The child is asked to spell, via jumping in squares, etc., a word that sounds the same but has a different meaning from the one placed on the blackboard or spelled out for him and pronounced (i.e., *bear, bare*).

Modifications: The child can be asked to think up pairs of words himself. One child can think up a word, and a second can think of a matching word.

GAME 113   Definitions

Equipment: Blackboard, letter squares

Method: A word is placed on the blackboard, and the child jumps its definition in squares. Or, the child is given the definition and then spells the answer by jumping into the proper squares in order.

Modifications: Words or definitions may be given orally rather than written on the board. Handicapped children can give answers by throwing bean bags.

GAME 114   Writing and Printing

Equipment: Letter squares, blackboard.

Method: A word is written on the board, and the child must jump appropriate letters in order on the larger squares. Writing is made in manuscript, but response is on printed letters, both upper- and lower-case.

Modifications: Manuscript letters on larger blocks may be obtained, and the child must find corresponding letters on other blocks containing printed letters (that is, first jump into one type of letter while spelling a word and then jump into the same letters in the other style). Proper names requiring upper-case letters should be used at times.

GAME 115   Musical Letters

Equipment: Letter squares arranged in large circles.

Method: Children walk around a circle outside letters, to music. They stop beside the nearest letter when the music stops, and they tell the name of the letter and make a word starting with that letter. Each time a letter is removed, so that there will be one fewer letter than children. The child left out each time is out of the game.

Modifications: The word to be thought of can be within a different announced category each time (for example, fruit, country, occupation). Words can also be used in a sentence.

GAME 116   See and Jump

Equipment: Flash cards containing printed words, squares containing pictures.

Method: Card, containing noun, is flashed. The child jumps into the square with the corresponding picture. Start with two possible squares, and then gradually increase the number of choices.

Modifications: Other responses can be used, such as hopping or skipping. The noun can be spoken (i.e., *boy, girl, ball*) and then the proper square jumped in.

GAME 117   Draw and Hop

Equipment: Blackboard, squares containing printed words, letter squares.

Method: One child can draw picture of something (for instance, a girl) on the board, and an observing child can then find the corresponding word shape. She jumps into the square containing the word shape and/or jumps through the correct letters, in order, in the letter grid.

Modifications: Competition can be introduced between two or more children observing the drawing.

GAME 118   Hop and Say

Equipment: Letter squares, flash cards containing pictures, and large jumping squares containing pictures of persons, places, and things.

Method: The child is given a word verbally (*boy*). He must find and jump into square containing picture that corresponds to that word, and then jump in the correct letters in order on the letter grid.

Modifications: A flash card containing pictures can be shown to the child, and then he may respond by hopping or jumping into appropriate squares of grid.

GAME 119   Steal the Word

Equipment: Words on large squares placed between two teams.

Method: Children on each team are given numbers starting with 1. A number is called, together with a word. The children with that number from each team attempt to retrieve the word called from the pile between the teams. The winner gets a point. The teacher should call "house-2" rather than "2-house" so all children think about the word.

Modifications: The word can be flashed and its match sought by each pair of children called.

GAME 120   Story Relays

Equipment: Blackboard, chalk.

Method: Choose two teams of ten or more children each. The first child on each team runs to the blackboard, begins a sentence, returns, tags the next child in order, and each child adds a word until all members are finished. They must form a coherent sentence or sentences. The first team finished wins.

Modifications: Children may race, using movements other than running. Sentences may be formed with cards containing words, rather than written on the blackboard one word at a time.

GAME 121   Read and Act

Equipment: Blackboard; flash cards containing verbs or verb phrases; letter, word, or number squares.

Method: A card is flashed, and the child must act out the verb, (for instance, run, jump, draw a circle, jump in a "cat," hop in an *A*). An observing child checks the appropriateness of the nature of the movement. If the child is correct, he may become a "teacher" and choose a new card. The child previously flashing the card becomes the performer. The procedure may be used with groups of three or more children—one a card flasher, the second an observer-scorer, and the third performing the movement.

Modifications: Competition may be set up between teams of children. Correct or incorrect scores determine the total team score. The game can start with an act (for instance, running) and then an attempt can be made to find the appropriate word.

GAME 122   Reading Directions

Equipment: Number, letter, and word squares, cards containing a series of directions (for example, run, jump, walk into a square).

Method: A child is given a card and a set period of time to read the directions. An observing child then takes the card. The first child acts out the directions and the observing child determines whether the first child is carrying out the directions in the correct order and appropriately.

Modifications: Four, five, or more directions can be given. Activities required can become progressively more difficult. Competition between two or more children, following the same or different directions, can be introduced, with the winner determined by accuracy and/or speed.

GAME 123   Matching Words

Equipment: Flash cards containing words, squares containing homonyms (that is, words with the same sound but with a different meaning and spelling), letter squares.

Method: Children must observe the flash card and then jump in, retrieve, or spell out a word that sounds the same but is different (for instance, *bear, bare; reed, read*).

Modifications: Words can be spoken in a sentence, either when presented or when matched. The words can be spoken singly and both alternatives (or three alternatives) spelled out.

GAME 124   Base Progress

Equipment: Cards containing vocabulary words, a three- or four-base game facility.

Method: Two teams alternate. The hitter on the up team must name the word flashed by a member of the other team. If he does, he may go to first base; if not, he is out (after five outs the other team is up). Members of the up team force one another around the bases and score runs when

forced home. The fielding team selects harder words to flash (or write on a board) as the game progresses.

Modifications: Children may run, hop, or otherwise negotiate the bases. Words flashed may indicate how a child may proceed from base to base (run, skip, walk, etc., giving help in verb recognition).

GAME 125   Reading Basketball

Equipment: Basketball hoop, balls, blackboard and/or flash cards containing vocabulary words.

Method: Two teams, each at a different basket, must name the words flashed (or written on the board) by a member of opposite team. If this is done, the team member gets to attempt a basket (point is scored if word is named correctly, and a second point is scored if the basket attempt is successful).

Modifications: Children who make a basket can move to different locations around the court to earn additional points. If only one basket is available, the

children can have an up team and a flashing (or writing) team. Shooting can be preceded by dribbling the ball.

GAME 126   Read, Pass, or Throw

Equipment: Footballs, blackboard or flash cards of vocabulary words to be learned, tape measures, playground balls, softballs, bean bags.

Method: Each child coming "up" is given a word (via a flash card or written on the blackboard). She must name it correctly, use it in a sentence, and then throw the football for distance. Points are scored according to distance thrown, whether word is correctly pronounced, and whether it is used in a sentence correctly. Points for throwing distance depend on age and ability level of the children.

Modifications: Children flashing cards or drawing words on the board check accuracy and may take the throwers' places if they are incorrect. Balls of various types may be thrown corresponding to ability, sex, physical disability, etc. Balls may be batted or kicked for distance, rather than thrown.

GAME 127   Obstacle Course Reading

Equipment: Tires, boxes, mats, tape, ropes, hoops.

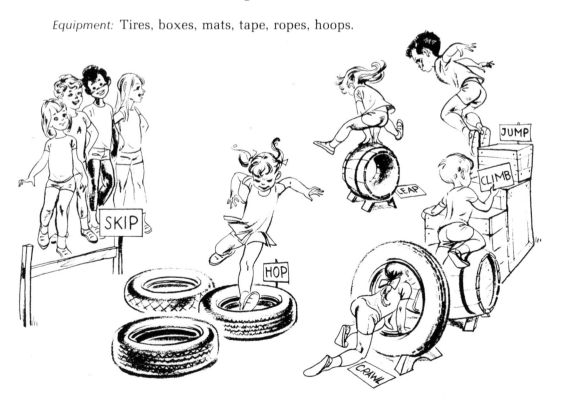

Method: A child may proceed through an obstacle course if he is able to read a new word placed on each obstacle. After each run-through, new words are placed on the obstacles. Team or individual competition can be introduced. Additional points for finishing time and/or the ability to use a word in a sentence can be given.

Modifications: The obstacle course may be made with lining tape, using two-dimensional obstacles rather than more elaborate three-dimensional obstacles. Children in wheelchairs may have "obstacles" in the form of things to throw bean bags into or over (scrap baskets, circles on the floor).

GAME 128   Write a Story

Equipment: Paper and pencil, equipment as needed.

Method: Classroom time is devoted to the assignment of writing a movement story. Playground time is then devoted to reading the story by other class members and carrying out activities as it is read.

Modifications: Reading may be done aloud accompanying movements. Stories may be reasonably complex and need not include the need for constant movement. A child may read the story silently and act out movements as needed.

GAME 129   Wait and Read

Equipment: Blackboard, flash cards containing words.

Method: One member at a time from two relay teams is required to read a word flashed (or written on a board). If she can, she may leave immediately on her relay trip; if not, she must delay one, two, or three seconds before starting. The trip can consist of dodging, running, etc. She returns to tap the next person, who is then shown the next word.

Modifications: If the word meaning can be supplied by the next team member in line, the starting penalty time may be reduced. If the word can be pronounced but not used in a sentence, more penalty time is introduced. If the word can be used in a sentence by the second teammate, the penalty time can be reduced.

GAME 130   Read and Run

Equipment: Room or athletic field, flash cards containing words.

Method: Place pairs of cards, each containing different words, one under the other at various stations in the room or on an athletic field. Children each start with a different "top" word and then quickly look underneath, finding the second different word, which they must then run and find as another top word. They then look underneath that third word, finding the next word to which they must run, etc.

Modifications: Individual children can be timed through the word obstacle course. Groups of children can go at once, each one trying to catch the next child. Words can be increasingly difficult. Children can be asked to make up a sentence on finding each word.

SUMMARY AND OVERVIEW

The games in this chapter and their modifications provide a wide variety of movement experiences through which children may acquire knowledge of the sounds and shapes of the intricate "visual templates" that appear in the form of letters and word-shapes. These enclosures of space confront children as they enter school and present significantly more sophisticated problems than they faced while playing with their friends before beginning classes.

The chapter begins with simple ways in which the child may be helped to organize letters' orientations—up and down, slanted, as well as difficult left-right asymmetries found in various letters. These games employ a coding concept, assuming that, just like the spy, the child is faced with the problem of breaking the letter-word-spatial-dimension codes contrived by the culture.

Other games that follow may be incorporated into school lessons or played during the school day and at other times and places considered appropriate by the teacher. Sometimes the grids are placed in parts of a classroom. At other times they may be placed on the playground. Some teachers project various grids and targets containing letters and words onto the floor or on the wall, using a slide projector. Another innovation employed is the rear-screen projector. Using this tool, children may interact with the grids and patterns without getting in the way of a projected image.

Many of the games contain opportunities for the child to write and to think sequentially and logically. Most of the games and modifications attempt to instill various word-attack skills, including the analysis of words—breaking them down into component parts, which may be sounded out.

The activities in this chapter integrate well into games found in the chapters dealing with mathematics, problem solving, memory, and the organization of space.

The various language-speech activities contained in the section that follows may also be integrated into the games in this chapter.

All of the games may be conducted with various numbers of children (from two to thirty or more), and they may also be practiced with children who have physical handicaps. More children may be involved than is sometimes indicated by the accompanying illustrations, if the teacher carefully organizes "learning teams," consisting of recorders, performers, and observers/evaluators. These roles must be shifted from time to time in order for optimum learning to take place. Nonambulatory physically handicapped children may become valuable and productive members of these "learning teams" if they are afforded opportunities to employ the physical responses available to them. Thus a jumping response may be translated into a throwing response or even into a simple placing response on the same grids that more physically robust children are jumping on.

BIBLIOGRAPHY

ASHER, J.J.   The strategy of the total physical response: An application to learning Russian. *International Review of Applied Linguistics*, 1965, 4, 291-300.

CHOMSKY, N.   Reading, writing and phonology. In M. Wolf, M. McQuillan, and E. Radwin (Eds.), *Thought and language/language and reading*. Cambridge, MA: Harvard Educational Review Reprint Series, 1980.

CRATTY, B.J.   *Coding games*. Denver: Love Publishing, 1981.

CRATTY, B.J., and MARTIN, SISTER M.M.   *The effects of learning games upon children with learning difficulties*. Los Angeles: UCLA, Dept. of Kinesiology, Monograph, 1971.

HENDRICKSON, L.N., and MUEHL, S.   The effects of attention and motor response pre-training on learning to discriminate b, d, in kindergarten children. *Journal of Educational Psychology*, 1962, *53*, 236-241.

HUMPHREY, J.   Comparison of the use of the active game learning medium with traditional procedures in the reinforcement of reading skills with fourth grade children. *Journal of Special Education*, 1967, *1*, 369-373.

JEFFREY, W.E.   Variables in early discrimination learning I. Motor responses in training a left-right discrimination. *Child Development*, 1958, *29*, 269-275.

MARCHANKS, G., and LEVIN H.   Cues by which children recognize words. *Journal of Education Psychology*, 1965, no. 2, 57-61.

THORNBURG, K.R., and FISHER, V.L.   Discrimination of 2-d letters by children after play with 2- or 3-d letter forms. *Perceptual and Motor Skills*, 1970, *30*, 979-986.

VAN OSDOL, R.M., JOHNSON, D.M., and GEIGER, L.   The effects of total body movement on reading achievement. *Australian Journal of Mental Retardation*, 1974, *3*, 16-19.

WATT, W.C., and JACOBS, D.   The child's conception of the alphabet. *Claremont Reading Conference, Bulletin*, 1975, 131-137.

CHAPTER 7

Communication: Talking and Writing

Children begin developing communications skills very early in their lives. Soon after birth, infants learn to communicate needs, emotions, and simple ideas to any adults patient and perceptive enough to understand. Within a few more months, the early babblings begin to form themselves into echoes of the voices of those crowding around the crib. Word learning progresses quickly, and it has been estimated that during the third and fourth years children acquire a new word-meaning every waking hour. This high rate of absorption signals an explosion of concepts, as children learn to recognize and to attach words to the objects, people, and circumstances in the world that surrounds them.

Written communication comes later. However, even during the first attempts at scribbling, which generally occur within the second year, children learn to communicate excitement and energy to those who observe. When children enter school, if environmental conditions have encouraged it, rudimentary printing and writing begin. By the end of the elementary school years children are able both to write complex stories and to retell them orally.

Both written and oral communication are closely interwoven with action. Writing *is* partly a motor task, and it involves both visual and auditory perception as well as intelligence. Verbal communication is at times inseparable from physical activity. Mothers of two- and three-year-olds use speech to encourage their children to move and to dissuade them from action. Later, according to perceptive research by Vygotsky (1962) and Luria (1961), children's efforts at movement are closely linked to their own private speech, uttered internally, as well as to sentences and words that are spoken out loud.

Speech pathologists and linguists, recognizing the close relation of action and speech-language functions, long ago began to use games in their therapy sessions and in their research (Curren and Cratty 1978). Some of those attempting to teach foreign languages, upon noting how quickly children learn a second tongue while playing, have promoted the use of a "total action response" when acquiring such difficult systems of words as are found in Russian and Japanese (Asher 1969).

Early in the life of infants the vocalizations of others apparently influence action. Voices spoken over the crib of the neonate may start or terminate what many believe to be random arm and leg movements. When infants are able to sit and to manipulate, movements are also linked to the words of others, although often with surprising and frustrating results. Research has indicated, for example, that an infant will continue a movement with more effort when first confronted with the word *stop*. Later, after maturation of the nervous system, the word *stop* will produce a looking response. Only later, hearing the word will bring the child to terminate the action to the command halt.

As the child begins to acquire speech and language[1] during the second year of life, even more interesting pairings of words and deeds are noted. First the child may seem to "pre-program" movements by saying, for example, "Now Johnny is going to bounce the ball." Such speech is often followed by the action paired with a present tense description of what is being done. The same child, for example, might bounce the ball, while saying for others to hear, "Now Johnny is bouncing the ball." At times an action is described in a loud voice after it has been completed—"Johnny has bounced the ball."

The child soon learns however, that it is often cumbersome to accompany actions with words that others can hear. Thus, speech becomes internalized or is whispered when an action is taking place.

Subvocal or internal speech is believed by many to enhance intellectual processes; often this type of language use is an important accompaniment to written communicative efforts. Thus the encouragement of both overt as well as covert language skills may have useful outcomes.

Language skills are generally classified into two primary categories:

(a) *Expressive language* consists of the words children speak so that others can hear while they construct thoughts in the form of words, sentences, and paragraphs.

(b) *Receptive language*, in contrast, reflects how well children perceive and understand what is spoken. Children having problems developing good expressive-language skills may not have problems understanding their native language and the reverse may also be true—children possessing good expressive-language skills may have a difficult time understanding others (Owens 1984).

---

[1]Speech is usually defined as having something to do with the articulation or enunciation of words—as more a motor skill than an intellectual operation. Language, on the other hand, is usually defined as the vocabulary and sentence content of what is being said. Language, therefore, is more conceptually based than is speech. For the most part, this chapter's activities focus upon language, not upon the improvement of speech.

The games and activities in this chapter reflect attempts to demonstrate how various forms of communication may be paired in effective ways with movement experiences. Games to enhance and encourage both internal as well as voiced speech-language are combined with those that focus upon written communication. Activities that contain both expressive and receptive-language components are also outlined.

Many of these activities may be integrated in useful ways with other games presented in previous parts of the text and especially with more presented in Chapter 6. The importance of understanding a language to learning to read it has already been explained.

Children's first vocal efforts often consist of what has been named a "showing schema." During the second year, infants often hold objects up for viewing, while at the same time giving them a name. Following this period, progress in language learning in normal children generally proceeds at a great rate. If a child is going to have difficulty learning language, this usually becomes apparent during this period. It is hoped that the games that follow sill suggest ways in which language skills and writing skills may be enhanced in normal youngsters, and that they will also suggest strategies useful to the parent or teacher trying to stimulate these same abilities in a typical children and youth (Garcia 1982).

GAME 131   Show and Say

Equipment: Large floor or matted area, box containing common objects (such as balls, spoons, small boxes, and the like).

Method: Children, in a group or individually, are shown an object, and the teacher/parent states its name. Child takes object and tries to name it also. With young children, an attempt is all that's necessary. (Often a two-to-three year old child will only utter the first sound.) It is best to start with objects named by words that begin with hard consonant sounds (for example, box, doll, etc.).

Show and say can continue with actions instead of being objects demonstrated by the teacher/parent, and then named. Child can attempt the action also, trying to name it before and/or after it is executed. Again, words beginning with a hard consonant sounds (for instance, clap, go, etc.) work best initially.

Modifications: More mature children may name the object and try to do something with it. The action may also be executed after the child names it, or one child can observe the action and hear it named, and then turn to a second child who has not observed the action and try to instruct him in what to do. Alternatively a child may be shown an object (a box or ball) and then upon hearing it named (or naming it herself) may proceed to try an action with the object, (for instance, bounce the ball). The action may also be named.

GAME 132   Do What I Say

Equipment: Large floor or matted area, on which the outlines of a house or barn are drawn or taped (see illustration). Barn may contain windows, doors, and the like together with animals' pictures. Implements such as, a bucket to feed the cow, or perhaps a watering can to water the "flowers" drawn near the house may also be included.

Method: This game, which involves receptive language, may start with teacher/parent instructions to go and/or to do something around the house or barn. These can include "Go out the door," "Water the flowers," "Look out the window," etc. As children progress, more complicated directions involving more than one action may be given. Other children evaluate "correctness" of the listener's responses.

Modifications: After teacher/parent directions, children may be encouraged to give each other directions and to evaluate "correctness" of outcomes. Directions may be progressive, with additions made one at a time. In this way, memory span may be tested. An entire story may be acted out in sequences, using the house or barn as a model.

GAME 133   Talk to Yourself!

Equipment: Floor or matted area, balls, ropes, and the like.

Method: This game, which involves self-administered directions, encourages self-talk of a useful kind, accompanying actions. Child is asked to first say what he is going to do. He should use the first person, "I", (for instance, "I am going to jump"). Next the child should jump and say what he is doing, using an "ing" continuous action verb modification ("I am jumping"). Finally, after the action is completed, child should voice aloud what he has just performed ("I jumped"). Actions involving regular rather than irregular verbs should be used if possible at first (that is, clap, clapping, clapped; *not* run, running, ran). Later irregular verbs and verb forms might be attempted.

Modifications: Discussion might take place as to whether it is easy to both perform and say what is being done at the same time. Alternative ways to accompany (or not accompany) speech with action might be explored. Additionally, children who are mature enough might discuss and discover how regular verbs are changed in order to indicate, present, past, future, and continuous actions. Other alternatives include having observing children voice what a performing child is doing—"John is going to jump," "John is jumping," John jumped"—with an effort made by other student-evaluators to determine (a) whether verb tenses are correctly used, and (b) whether actions being spoken about are being performed.

GAME 134   Say and Whisper

Equipment: Blackboard, ropes, balls, and the like, floor space or matted area.

Method: Children are asked to state what movement they are about to do before doing it. Next they are asked to say what they are doing while they are doing it. Finally they are asked to describe the action after performing it. This may be followed by a discussion about the efficiency of talking while acting. "Can you become confused if the skill is fast, and your words cannot keep up?"

Next the children, one at a time, attempt to reduce whole sentences describing a movement into sentence fragments. These fragments may be used before, during, and after a movement is performed.

Finally, whispered sentence or sentence fragments are used before, during, and after a movement has been performed. Discussions may then be held, and trials made, concerning the advantages and disadvantages of talking before, during, and after movements. The uses of sentences, fragments of sentences, and whispered sentence fragments may be tried out with movements of varying degrees of complexity and of various speeds.

Modifications: Children may be asked to write sentences or sentence fragments on the board. Contrasts between external and internal speech may be attempted using various kinds of movements. Movements that are complex and just being learned may be attempted with and without accompanying vocalization. New movements may be introduced, and the children asked to move from voiced sentences to sentence fragments to whispers and finally to subvocal internal speech.

Young children attempting to expand their language skills, language-deficient children, and children with motor problems and/or attentional problems may also benefit from this game.

GAME 135   Watch and Tell Another

Equipment: Chairs facing away from and toward an activity area, blackboard, balls, hoops, ropes, and other equipment as needed.

Method: Children are divided into groups, each consisting of a performer, an observer, and one who has her back to the initial action. Other roles may include recorders as well as evaluators. Before one child performs, another observing child is asked to (a) watch what is about to take place, and (b) tell the child who cannot view the action what the performing child did. The action performed should be simple at first (for instance, bouncing a ball once). Next the nonviewer turns around and tries to duplicate the action demonstrated. Evaluators assess the accuracy of what the nonviewer did, based upon the initial demonstration/performance. Children may change roles. Discussions afterwards may involve such topics as whether one-way communication or two-way communication is best ("Should the nonviewer ask questions?" "What about written communication?" and the like). Make sure those explaining the movement performed to a nonviewer do not use gestures.

Modifications: Nonverbal communication may be contrasted to verbal communication as explainer may or may not be permitted to use gestures or demonstration. Two-way communications and conversations between viewer and nonviewers may be attempted, and in the discussion that follows the merits of one-way vs. two-way communications may be discussed. Poor evaluations may be followed by additional trials that experiment with both verbal and written (that is notes) communication.

GAME 136   Add To . . .

Equipment: Blackboard, writing materials, balls, hoops, and other playground and play equipment.

Method: To enhance memory for verbal communication, a demonstrator should perform a movement at a specific location defined as one among several taped to the ground, as shown. Observers are then to inform nonobservers of what they are to do. A second movement is added to the first by the performer; these two are then described to nonobservers, who try to perform both movements in series. This is continued using three or more movements and figures. Thus descriptions must include what movement, with what implement (ball, etc.), as well as at what location.

Modifications: Written communication may be used in the same way as is verbal communication. The nonobserver must remember what is written. A single movement may be made more complex at the same location or a single movement may be performed in several locations, which must be described. Experimentation may be attempted with both brief and lengthy descriptions and with both one-way and two-way communication. That is, the nonobserver may or may not ask questions during verbal communications that describe movement(s).

GAME 137 Write and Do

Equipment: Blackboard, writing paper, desks, playground equipment, balls, hoops, ropes, and the like.

Method: Child demonstrates a movement or a series of two or three movements. Observing children begin to write about what has been done in order to communicate the movement(s) to nonobservers. Next, nonobservers try to replicate the action or actions of the first demonstrator, with their success rated by observers. Degree of success determines whether a new movement is to be demonstrated and described in written form in the same way, or whether the initial movement may be described in better detail, using additional written communication.

Modifications: Chains of communicators, consisting of three or more written communicators, may describe a movement and then try to change the written description while retaining the essence of the movement. Written communication may be alternated with verbal communication in such chains. Written communication of a movement may be attempted with as few words as possible. Movements may be started with written descriptions, and then the movement may follow. Children may write a "motor story," consisting of instructions for various actions to be carried out, and depicting various characters in the story, meanings of the story, or emotions within the story.

GAME 138 Rules

Equipment: Blackboard, writing materials, as well as balls and other playground equipment, and "junk equipment."

Method: The purpose of the game is to write rules that will clearly describe a new game or modification of a traditional game. The description should be attempted by one designated team of children, or youth, and a second team may then try to play it. Thought should be given to what kinds of rules many games, if not most games, have (for example, rules about stopping, starting, scoring, fouls, players, space, energy, and the like). Teams may change roles—from rule writers to players. Evaluators should determine what games are the most interesting and which one is described best. Experimentation may take place with writing established rules for known games and with making up entirely new rules. Teams making up rules should experiment with passive vs. active writing; that is, whether it is easier to first try out a new game or to first make it up passively on paper before presenting the rules to others.

Modifications: Modifications of historical games may be attempted in written form. Games reflecting various cultures may be written out and attempted. One team may silently make up a game by just playing it and experimenting with it physically. A second, observing team may then attempt to "codify" it in the form of written rules. Transmission of a new or modified game may take place with both verbal and written communication. Rules may be given all at once to a playing team, in writing or verbally, or they may be added as the playing team confronts needs for the rules.

GAME 139   Trust and Movement

Equipment: A safe obstacle course made up of harmless obstacles—boxes, rubber traffic markers, and the like (as shown).

Method: A child is blindfolded and attempts to proceed from one end of an obstacle course to the other, depending upon verbal directions given by another child. Observers judge the adequacy of the directions, as well as the accuracy of the individual negotiating the obstacle course while listening to the directions. Directions may be given in advance (to test auditory memory) or given while the child is in the course. Competition may be instituted, and the obstacle course changed, as child negotiating course trades roles with the child giving directions.

Modifications: Experimentation with partial predirections vs. directions given while negotiating the course may be carried out. More than one child may negotiate the course at the same time, with the object being to study confusion of directions given simultaneously. Trials at various speeds may be attempted, while obstacle courses of varying lengths and of varying difficulty may also be experimented with. The blindfolded child may progress only by asking questions of those who are observing.

SUMMARY AND OVERVIEW

The activities in this chapter may be used to enhance various kinds of communication. Suggestions within the "modifications" sections are intended to aid teachers and parents in adjusting these activities to individual differences encountered both within typical and atypical populations. Some of the games also permit the expansion of communicative skills among creative and/or gifted youngsters who may wish to expand their horizons within a context provided by childhood games.

BIBLIOGRAPHY

ASHER, J.J. The total physical response technique of learning. *Journal of Special Education*, 1969, *3*, 45-52.

CURREN, J., and CRATTY, B.J. *Speech and language problems in children: A manual for parents and teachers.* Denver: Love Publishing, 1978.

GARCIA, E.E. Language acquisition: Phenomenon, theory, research. In B. Spodek (Ed.), *Handbook of research in early childhood education.* New York: MacMillan Free Press, 1982, 47-64.

LURIA, A.R. *The role of speech in the regulation of normal and abnormal behavior.* New York: Pergamon, 1961.

OWENS, R.E. *Language development: An introduction.* Columbus, OH: Charles E. Merrill, 1984.

VYGOTSKY, L.S. *Thought and language* (E. Haufmann and G. Vakar eds. and trans.). Cambridge, MA: M.I.T. Press, 1962 (originally published in 1934).

CHAPTER 8

Challenging Games
For Creative Youth

The attempt to identify the qualities that place some children higher on scales of intellectual and creative endeavor than others has occupied psychologists and educators for decades. Interest in measures of intelligence spurred a parallel search for indices of giftedness in the first several decades of this century. More recently, psychologists have turned their interest toward understanding the qualities that underlie creative ability; finding that creativity and high scores in intelligence tests do not always coincide (Getzels and Jackson 1962). Torrance (1979), for example, found that if one identified the gifted youths within a population of children scoring within the upper 20 percent in an intelligence test, it would be likely that about 70 percent of those scoring highest in a test of creative thinking would not be included in the first, so-called intellectually superior group.

An even more recent trend in the identification of "special children of promise" has been signalled by attempts to select children who are talented (Taylor 1968). One modern model suggests that most individuals exhibit talent in at least one of six fields of endeavor. These include (a) academic talent (b) creative talent (c) wisdom (d) planning abilities (e) prediction and forecasting, and (f) communicative abilities.[1]

These vigorous excursions into evaluation of superior qualities in children have not always been accompanied by equally industrious efforts to formulate curricula that encourage these qualities, nor by the training of

---

[1] A gifted child is usually defined as simply one who scores well above the mean on a standard test of intelligence, often over 130 or 140 I.Q. Creative thinking was evaluated on tests appearing in the 1960s, which usually attempted to evaluate a child's ability to perceive elements of the world in new combinations, involving the ability to combine two or more previously unassociated things, ideas, or events. Talent refers to the straightforward ability to perform well in a number of areas such as music, art, etc.

teachers to challenge the gifted, creative, and talented youngster to exhibit his best efforts (Taylor 1961).

Qualities that are likely to be exhibited by creative and talented children include many seen in the gifted, but in addition they include the tendency to search for new and unusual solutions to problems and to take intellectual risks. Creative and talented children tend to be venturesome in including new elements within their worlds. Often these traits do not earn them favorable social reactions within traditionally managed classrooms, and even less favorable receptions await them at the hands of ultra-conservative and structured physical educators. Creative children often come from homes in which parents are secure in their own expanding creative energies and are uncritical of original thinking on the part of their children. Thus this youngster is often confused when attempting to "operate" within home and school environments that contrast markedly with one another.

Both gifted and creative children are flexible and fluent with both ideas and words. They are able to identify problems and to tolerate at least moderate ambiguity. The work habits of these youngsters are often intense, as they make every effort to acquire a great deal of data —information that they can later examine, manipulative, place in new combinations, and modify.

At times their "road of life" is rough. Their tendency to be individualistic often results in their being labelled "rebellious" by caretaking teachers. The strain of attempting to reconcile the mundane realities of their social and educational environment with their rich, sophisticated, and usually complicated mental lives may result in undue tensions at school and at play (Burnside 1942; Taylor 1961).

The development and expansion of the qualities of gifted and creative children may not proceed evenly. Typically, according to those who have evaluated these youngsters (Torrance 1968), there is a lag somewhere about the ninth or tenth year of life. This has been attributed to the possibility that the pressures of peers and the lack of inspiring educational offerings somehow combine in ways that block their best efforts.

Often the social stresses placed upon gifted and creative children prompt them to mask their talents in a number of ways. They may become energetic social leaders, rather than concentrating upon their academic efforts; or they may rebel, and become nonconforming individuals whose behaviors serve no useful ends (Khatena 1982).

Gifted, creative, and talented children and youth are those who are able to make differences in society as they mature. Moreover their gifts, creative energies, and talents deserve as much effort, planning, and thought on the part of those planning school programs as is expended upon those who are less fortunate. Gifted children are often more vigorous socially and physically than are their less well-endowed classmates (Terman 1926). It has been a consistent finding that intellectually able children are above average in physical development (Dehan 1957; Walker 1966; Klausmeier 1958). In school settings the gifted and creative youngster is far more likely to participate in competitive athletics and to be successful on school teams. Thus the stereotype of the shy, unfit, and nonphysical but intellectually well-endowed child is difficult to reconcile with contemporary research findings.

Most important, it has been found that the preferred "learning style" of these exceptional youngsters involves movement experiences, rather than a style marked by passivity and listening (Dunn and Price 1980). Thus the justification for vigorous and yet challenging games within their school program seems apparent (Hermelin and O'Connor 1980).

This profile of creative and intellectually able youngsters as energetic and willing to move and to think while playing would seem to suggest curricula that are equally active and imaginative. And yet, even at this late date, it is difficult to locate books of activities well suited to these extremely able youngsters. Likewise absent from the literature are descriptions of vigorous ways for these children to pursue academic work in an environment that provokes intellectual curiosity.[2]

The activities suggested in this chapter are not meant only for the hypothetical few—the elite—whose levels of creativity and/or intellectual attainment have been identified in tests. Rather, these games are intended to "tap into" the creative and intellectual energies of all children. For, as has been pointed out, virtually every child is talented in at least one area of endeavor; and those who haven't been identified as such have likely not encountered challenging educational experiences within the proper accepting school and/or home environments.

The games in this chapter are not a complete offering of what might be termed a physical education program for creative/gifted/talented children. A complete program of this type would offer such children opportunities to explore physiology by examining the processes that change as the result of exercising their own bodies; and to understand the physics of the efforts they make in sports and games. What follows is a sampling of what might be included in a challenging physical education program for all children, or conversely, of what might be included as "moving parts" of an academic program for children and youth who need to be challenged.

GAME 140   Codes

Equipment: Balls, ropes, matted area, floor space, blackboard, junk and real equipment.

Method: Following a discussion of what a "code" is, and how they are used by spies, the children are introduced to various codes used in school such

---

[2]And yet at least one test purports to evaluate creative thinking with games! (Torrance 1968).

as ways of classifying chemicals and formulas, names for the species and classes of animals, number codes to indicate quantity, and letter and word codes to indicate ideas and permit us to communicate. Next, children are shown how various configurations (for instance, symbols on the blackboard) may represent various movements or movement classifications. A team is formed to formulate a three-symbol code, with each symbol (letter, figure, etc.) indicating a different movement. After the team decides on the symbol-to-movement pairings, they present it to a second team, which attempts to break the code, while watching the first team move in ways indicated by the symbols the members of the first team write on the blackboard. Next the teams form codes in which a given symbol stands for some classification (or type) of movement (for example, an R might stand for a movement with a ball). Each symbol is then performed by the code-making team (an R written on the board might then be reacted to in any number of ways, just so that a ball is used). After forming and performing this movement-classification of movement code (usually 3 to 4 symbols is best at first), a second team tries to break the code, while watching the movements performed and observing the symbols written on the board. The game is reversed and the second team makes up a new symbol code. Balls and ropes may be used in movement responses.

Modifications: Sounds may be used instead of written symbols to indicate movements or classifications of movement. A symbol-to-sound-to-movement, three-part code may be formulated and then broken by an observing team. Movements that stand for letters or words may result in secret messages being given, messages that need to be "intercepted" by observing opponents of the "spies" formulating the code.

GAME 141   Equipment Invention

Equipment: Junk equipment, handicraft supplies, foam rubber or plastic forms, traditional game equipment.

Method: Children are introduced to discussion of the equipment found in traditional games (such as basketball), as well as facilities, markings, goals, and the like. Their job is to invent new equipment to be used in games, equipment that they may build (for instance, balls with new shapes, courts with new dimensions, and other such things possible to construct). Next they are to invent a new game or a new form of an old game that uses this equipment, and to try it out. Try-outs should be followed by further equipment, court, and facility modifications, and

Further ideas may be obtained in B.J. Cratty, *Coding games* (Denver: Love Publishers, 1981).

by further experimentation with the equipment and the game forms they suggest. Often cooperation of school workshops are useful and necessary in this project.

Modifications: Games in two dimensions may be thought about and designed (drawn) in three dimensions, or even four dimensions!(time). Equipment may be "invented" from prior environments (for example, kitchens, garden, etc.) to be used in traditional games. A playground's climbing apparatus is ideal in this context. The design and partial construction of an ideal playground can result from a project like this. A drafting teacher may be a useful partner in this latter project.

GAME 142 Combinations

Equipment: Balls, ropes, and other traditional game equipment; writing paper, desks, blackboards, game areas, tape and/or lining equipment; ropes to make boundaries.

Method: This game involves the synthesis of, or putting together of, parts of two or more traditional games. First the children are encouraged to analyze traditional games—their intent, rules, and general game forms. Next, either while thinking and/or while experimenting physically, the children are asked to make up a new game by combining the parts of two or more games. Thus, a game combining basketball and volleyball might be formulated, involving combinations of rules, equipment (that is, net and baskets), etc. A creative name may be invented (for instance, BASKVOL). The new game may then be tried out, taught to others, and refined further as "bugs" are discovered when it is played. The children might to try to find games around the world that seem to combine games that they know (for instance, Australian Rules Football). They might try to discover the historical antecedents of contemporary games, showing how their parts evolved and combined.

Modifications: The game invented may be described with written rules. The game may be invented and modified to suit children of various ages. The parts of the games that have been combined that were *not* used in the invented game may also be combined to constitute still another game.

For further suggestions see C.B. Corbin, *Inexpensive equipment for games, play, and physical activity* (Dubuque, IA: Brown and Co., 1972); and P.H.J. Werner and R.A. Simmons, *Inexpensive physical education equipment* (Minneapolis: Burgess Co., 1976).

For further suggestions on this and other activities discussed in this chapter consult B.J. Cratty, *Intelligence in action* (Englewood Cliffs, NJ: Prentice-Hall, 1975).

GAME 143 Video-Game: Explorer's Treasure

Equipment: A circular maze is drawn as shown, on blacktop taped on the floor of a gymnasium, lined on the lawn. or made with ropes on the floor.

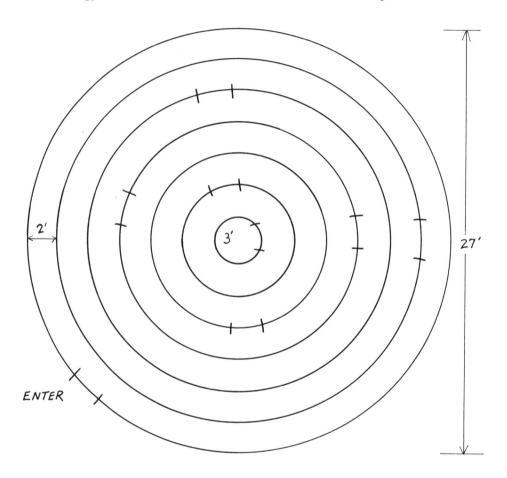

Method: The object is for an explorer to enter the maze, proceed to the middle, obtain the treasure, and return, without being captured (touched) by the roving guardians of the treasure. Guardians move at a constant rate, indicated by a musical beat or a metronome, and walk around the rings guarding the treasure. If they encounter the explorer, they touch her, and prevent her from reaching the treasure (explorer must return to the "outside world" if touched.) Explorer(s) is (are) safe when reaching the center circle with the treasure, but may be captured upon return. Beat that guardians walk while the explorer enters the maze may differ from beat they walk when she exits. Children may compete individually or in teams, with criteria for judging winning being not only amount of treasure (gold painted rocks) seized, but the time needed to seize the treasure. Maze may be enlarged or reduced in size. Passage may be made only through gates indicated on circular rings.

Modifications: Two explorers may enter at the same time, or at different times. Guardians may have different timed movement programs; circles (containing guards) may be reduced, or increased. Restrictions may be placed on how long an explorer may remain in the maze, safe with the treasure, or on total time of traversal. Various restrictions may be placed on movements of the explorer. Guardians may creep, if the surface is grassy or if it is matted, as may explorer. One or more guard per ring may be used.

GAME 144   Video-Game: The Jungle Pathway

Equipment: A lined area (as shown) indicating a jungle pathway—straight or curved—with various caves and swamps indicated in which animals and other dangers hide.

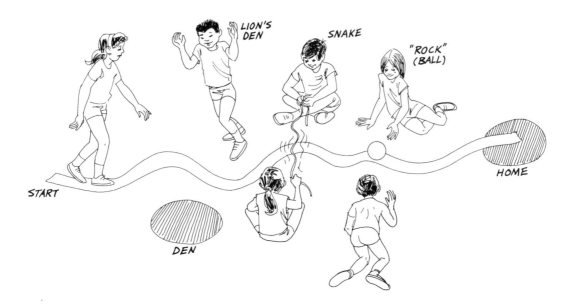

Method: The object of this game is for "Jungle Boy/Girl" to get safely down the jungle path without encountering (touching) any of the "wild things" (played by other children) that frequently pass across the path. Three or more "wild things" are "programmed" to move with a constant speed, back and forth across the path, from their hiding places on either side of the path. Their speeds may be made to vary, depending upon movement restrictions placed on them. "Jungle Boy/Girl" must get down the path without meeting the "wild things." "Wild things" might include: A lion who skips back and forth from his den; a wild-child who bounces a ball back and forth across the path; a snake who slithers across the path (a rope, held at either end, made to "slither" back and forth as ends are moved rapidly); a rock that rolls across the path (ball rolled from child to child, across the jungle path); other "obstacles" as needed and invented.

Modifications: New obstacles may be added as needed and wanted. Jungle boys and girls may be given latitude to run fast, walk, etc. Three dimensional obstacles may be used, (for instance, hills, rocks to climb over, boxes, etc.). Game may be played in flat outdoor areas, hilly-forest areas, and/or matted gymnasium areas, with or without equipment. Space left in path, to be broadjumped, may reflect a canyon to be crossed.

GAME 145   Video-Game: Prisoner's Maze

Equipment: "Maze," as shown, made in grassy area (boundaries made with nylon boat line "nailed" to ground), or on pavement (with permanent or temporary lines).

Method: This chase-and-tag, "video-like" game is played with two or more members at a time. All must stay on pathways that form grid, with "safe" areas designated at several (or all) small squares formed by intersecting pathways (areas in which "escaping prisoner" may not be tagged).

A prisoner, one at a time, tries to escape from the dungeon at the top of the maze, while guards try to prevent escape by touching prisoner while she is in the maze. Guards' movements are restricted to a walk in cadence to a metronome (or music) beat. Walk involves keeping at least one foot in contact with the ground at all times. Game may be made more difficult or easier, with grids of various sizes, increasing or decreasing numbers of guards, and/or various levels of restrictions on movements of guards or escaped prisoners (for instance, may be held to hopping, jumping with two-foot take-off and landing, etc.). Prisoner may be given freedom to run, walk, etc. to afford more or less difficult "capture." Competition may be carried out using team or individual scores. Method of capture may also vary, involving one or more guards to capture the escaping prisoner. Guards and prisoners must stay between lines forming grid, as indicated.

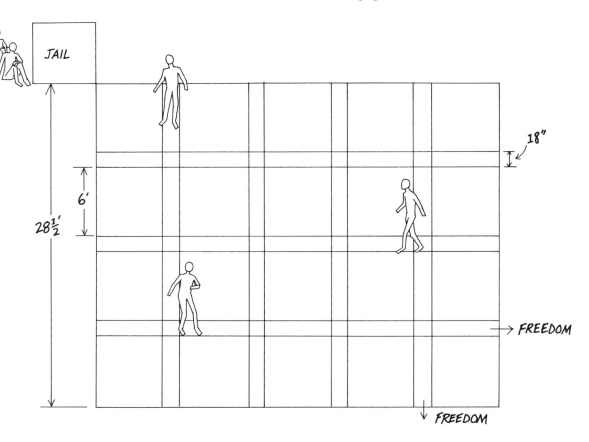

Modifications: Physically handicapped youngsters with various movement capacities may be included. Guards may be blindfolded and made to walk between channels formed by raised guardrails.

GAME 146   Video-Game: "Tron" Dodge-Ball

Equipment: A court outlined as follows, with approximate dimensions as shown; soft air-filled balls of 8 in. diameters, scoring blackboard.

Method: One child ("Tron") stands in the middle circle, while others at the periphery hurl rocket blasters (balls) at "Tron." Balls may be rolled, bounced two or three times, or thrown. Two balls may be projected at a time, but only one may be thrown (with no bounces) at a time. Children at periphery must be designated primary or secondary "rocket launchers" ("primary launchers" may throw ball directly, while "secondary launchers" may only roll or bounce balls at "Tron"). Object

is to score hits on "Tron" while he dodges to prevent being touched. Hits from bounced or rolled balls score two points more than hits from balls thrown with no bounce. Children alternate in center for a given time period (one to two minutes), with scores kept indicating number of hits. Low-scoring child wins. If "Tron" only dodges balls, launchers score no points against "Tron"; but if "Tron" hits incoming rockets with fist, he reduces point total by one for each hit.

Modifications: With younger children only one ball may be launched at a time. Experiment with distance and size dimensions of circle. Two "Trons" may be in center circle, one designated as rocket blaster (may hit incoming rockets with fists), while other is a rocket dodger (must avoid contact with "rockets" coming in).

GAME 147   Handicapping, Adapting

Equipment: Playground equipment, markings on asphalt, grassy area with marking equipment available, balls of various sizes.

Method: The object of this game is to take a traditional game (for example, volleyball or baseball), and scale it down so that children of various ages and/or talents may play. A game may be scaled down into two, three, or more levels suitable for children 3, 6, 8, etc. The game in its simplest form may be tried with younger children. Their comments may then be solicited for modifications. Children may read books describing lead-up games for ideas, as well as child-motor-development texts to ascertain what skills are needed at various levels. Skill testing and game try-outs may be held for research needed to formulate various levels of a game.

Modifications: A simple elementary school game may be scaled upward in difficulty to prove challenging to older children and youth. The game forms developed may be written up for elementary school curriculum guides. Different components of a difficult game may be scaled down in separate game forms, requiring less vigor, and involving easier rules, fewer people, and/or a different and simpler court or play-field area. Adaptations for handicapped children may be formulated.

GAME 148   Many Ways, the Best Way

Equipment: Balls, ropes, blackboard, matted surfaces, floor.

Method: This activity serves as an introduction to the concepts of divergent and convergent production (also called divergent and convergent thinking). Children are first told that they will be shown various ways to think, using the mat. Divergent thinking (finding many right or correct answers to a single problem) is explained. Then they are asked to demonstrate divergent thinking by going down the mat "as many ways as you can think of." Next they are introduced to the concept of convergent thinking (or production) involving problems in which a single or best answer to a problem is sought and arrived at. Then they are given specific directions as to how to go down the mat (for instance, "move with your back nearest the mat, but not touching, backwards your head goes first toward me, and only two feet, and one hand should be touching the mat"). Children can then find and try out various directions that are likely to elicit either divergent or convergent responses in movement, and various degrees of convergent or divergent thinking and behaviors (by means of semi-restrictive directions). Balls, ropes, and other equipment may also be used.

Modifications: Discussions and experimentation with traditional games that involve both restrictive rules (requiring a best, convergent response) and less-restrictive components (requiring divergent production) may take

For further suggestions see B. J. Cratty, *Perceptual and motor development in infants and children* (Englewood Cliffs, NJ: Prentice-Hall, 1979); _____, *Educational games for the physically handicapped* (Denver: Love Publishers, 1975); R. Volpe, *Lead-up games* (Englewood Cliffs, NJ: Prentice-Hall, 1965).

place. The children and youth may determine how they might make various games more or less restrictive. Additional discussion might deal with convergent and divergent production in the classroom (convergent thinking is frequently called for in the sciences, and divergent in the arts).

GAME 149   Feelings and Behaviors in Games

Equipment: Play area, scoring sheets.

Method: Children/youth are introduced to the concept of analyzing how people feel by observing their own behaviors toward each other. The behavior to be observed in this instance is how often players in a game pass to each member of the team. Speculation is made before and after a game concerning what the students think about friendship patterns on the team. The children/youth formulate (or are provided) with a score sheet, permitting them to mark how many times each player (a basketball-team game is best) passes to every other player. After watching a game, a practice, or portion of a game-practice, the children's scores are inspected to see if some kind of bias is seen in who passes to whom. Discussion that follows might focus upon what the children believe about (a) friendship and liking (and disliking) patterns on the team they observed and (b) how the biases they may have observed have either aided or hurt the team's performances. Discussion of influences of liking and disliking on other work-groups might also take place.

Modifications: With careful guidance, the children/youth might be encouraged to diagram what they believe are friendship patterns on the team observed. Additional discussion and experimentation might revolve around what other feelings among athletic teams and athletes influence production and performance of the team and of individuals.

SUMMARY AND OVERVIEW

The activities in this chapter have included those that capitalize upon the current interest in video-games by "enlarging" some of the concepts and techniques involved in those games in active and thought-provoking ways. The

For further suggestions see B.J. Cratty, *Learning about human behavior through active games* (Englewood Cliffs, NJ: Prentice-Hall, 1978). For suggestions on how to adapt for the more mature see B.J. Cratty (with R. Pigott), *Student projects in sport psychology* (Ithaca, NY: Mouvement Publications, 1984).

games in this chapter may also serve to stimulate creative and gifted children to think carefully and inventively. Some of the games also include enlargement on the "coding game" theme found in other parts of the text. Indeed, some bright youngsters might be encouraged to translate parts of the school curriculum or various cognitive operations (other than divergent or convergent thought) into coding games. The potential is unlimited.

There are many other types of activities involving movement that may be tried out with success on creative children. After teaching them muscle names and muscle actions, they might formulate exercise programs intended to exercise all parts of their bodies. Following a lecture and discussion on cardio-respiratory function, the same children or youth should be able to design an exercise program intended to make their lung-heart system more efficient. Indeed it will be found that children who have designed their own programs in this manner will participate in those programs with great gusto.

The video-game "theme" found in several of these games may be expanded upon in many ways. Creative children and youth may translate their favorite arcade games to vigorous games that may be practiced on the playground or in the gymnasium. If they seek to do this, encourage it!

BIBLIOGRAPHY

BURNSIDE, L.   Psychological guidance of the gifted. *Education*, 1942, 6, 223-228.

CORBIN, C.B.   *Inexpensive equipment for games, play and physical activity.* Dubuque, IA: Brown and Co., 1972.

CRATTY, B.J.   Intelligence and intelligence testing. Chapter 3 in my *Physical expressions of intelligence.* Englewood Cliffs, NJ: Prentice-Hall, 1973.

_____.   *Intelligence in action.* Englewood Cliffs, NJ: Prentice-Hall, 1975a.

_____.   *Educational games for the physically handicapped.* Denver: Love Publishing, 1975b.

_____.   *Learning about human behavior through active games.* Englewood Cliffs, NJ: Prentice-Hall, 1978.

_____.   *Perceptual and motor development in infants and children.* Englewood Cliffs, NJ: Prentice-Hall, 1979.

_____.   *Coding games.* Denver: Love Publishing, 1981.

CRATTY, B.J. (with PIGOTT, R).   *Student projects in sport psychology.* Ithaca, NY: Mouvement Publications, 1984.

DEHAN, R.F.   *Educating gifted children.* Chicago: Univ. of Chicago Press, 1957.

DREWS, E.M.   The four faces of able adolescents. *Saturday Review*, 1963, 46, 68-71.

DUNN, R.S., and PRICE, G.E.   The learning style characteristics of gifted students. *Gifted Child Quarterly*, 1980, 24, 33-36.

GALTON, F.   *Hereditary genius: An inquiry into its causes and consequences.* London: MacMillan, 1892.

GETZELS, J.W., and JACKSON, P.W.   *Creativity and intelligence: Explorations with gifted children.* New York: John Wiley, 1962.

GOWAN, J.C.   Background and history of the gifted-child movement. In J.C. Stanley and W.C. George (Eds.), *The gifted and creative: A fifty-year perspective, 1925-75.* Baltimore: Johns Hopkins Univ. Press, 1976.

HERMELIN, B., and O'CONNOR, N.   Perceptual, motor and decision speeds in specifically and generally gifted children. *Gifted Child Quarterly,* 1980, *24,* 56-61.

KHATENA, J.   *Educational psychology of the gifted.* New York: John Wiley, 1982.

KLAUSMEIER, H.J.   Physical, behavioral and other characteristics of higher and lower achieving children, in favored environments. *Journal of Educational Research,* 1958, *51,* 573-582.

TAYLOR, C.W.   Be talent developers as well as knowledge dispensers. *Today's Education,* 1968, *57,* 67-69.

————.   Finding the creative. *Science Teacher,* 1961, *28,* 593-606.

TERMAN, L.J.   *Mental and physical traits of a thousand gifted children: Genetic studies of genius.* Palo Alto, CA: Stanford Univ. Press, Vol. I, 1926.

TORRANCE, E.P.   A longitudinal examination of the fourth grade slump in creativity. *Gifted Child Quarterly,* 1968, *12,* 195-199.

————.   *Thinking creatively in action and movement.* Bensenville, IL: TCAM Scholastic Testing Service, 1978.

————.   Unique needs of the creative child and adult. In A.H. Passow (Ed.), *The gifted and talented: Their education and development.* Chicago: Univ. of Chicago Press, 1979.

VOLPE, R.   *Lead-up games.* Englewood Cliffs, NJ: Prentice-Hall, 1965.

WALKER, A.S.   *A comparative study of the physical fitness of special, average, and gifted twelfth-grade boys.* Eugene: Univ. of Oregon, M.S. thesis, 1966.

WERNER, H., and SIMMONS, R.A.   *Inexpensive physical education equipment for children.* Minneapolis: Burgess, 1976.

CHAPTER 9

And So . . .

The games in this book make up a "cafeteria" of possibilities from which teachers of both special and typical children and youth may choose. In general, classroom teachers will find it most useful to devote one, two, or three sessions per week to "activating" the curriculum. Some teachers of the very young may spend more time with the games, as may some instructors of hyperactive or easily distracted youngsters. Though illustrations to some of the games depict only a few participants, innovative teachers may involve larger numbers of children by arranging materials and facilities in creative ways.

Discussions of many of the activities include references to various thought processes that have been identified by both scientists and philosophers interested in cognitive-intellectual abilities and their development. One game in the previous chapter, for example, deals with both *divergent* and *convergent production*; while an entire chapter (3) contains games intended to improve *memory*. Other games include tasks intended to heighten children's abilities to *evaluate*, as well as active ways to improve their abilities to *classify*, or *categorize*. Some of the games, including several of the "coding" activities, require children to take apart more complex stimuli, and/or movements—that is, to *analyze*; while other games require children to build up a complex whole by combining component parts—that is, to *synthesize*. Several of the methods and modifications suggest that children, after analyzing some process, reverse the order of events. The importance of the ability to engage in this *reversibility* process has been identified by several "cognitive theorists," including Piaget (1965).

Transfer. The ability of the teacher to "tap into" these and other intellectual processes is dependent upon his willingness to enlarge his own knowledge of the process of knowledge acquisition itself. The methods by which these various processes are transferred from movement games to other tasks also need careful consideration and study. Both the methods and the modifications section of many of the games discuss ways in which this transfer may be accomplished. In order that transfer can occur, it is important (a) that the skill to be transferred be practiced frequently in its game application before the transfer to an academic application is attempted, and (b) that the teacher build "cognitive bridges" of understanding that involve both of the two tasks between which it is desired that transfer should occur. For example, it is often helpful, in trying to help children correct left-right confusions over the arrangement of left-right asymmetrical letters, to have them learn the left-right dimensions of their own bodies. Games and exercises that include opportunities to deal with the left-right orientations of their bodies (such as games that require that they distinguish between left and right body parts, that they recognize whether objects are to the left or right of them, lying down on their left or right sides, etc.) can assist in this first stage. Once this stage has been mastered, its lessons can be applied to mastering the second stage. When teaching a child that the E opens to the right, have her place her right hand on the page or directly on the right side of the E; or when teaching her that the straight line of the D goes on the left side, have her reach out with her left hand and touch the page and the "straight up line" of the D.

Aiding children to learn about how they may enhance memory in the ways suggested in Chapter 3 must also be built upon these same two principles of transfer. Children must, using movement tasks, learn in several ways (including visualization, association, etc.) how memory may be enhanced. Then the teacher should point out in exact ways, using academic materials to be memorized, just how these same retention aids will help memorization in other classroom contexts.

FREEDOM TO THINK

The activities in the preceding chapters are presented in ways that encourage participating children and youth to make various decisions about the formulation and modifications of those activities and to evaluate the quality of their peers' efforts at thoughtful action, after the outcomes of games are observed.

Some of the descriptions suggest that, after youthful participants become familiar with both the game and its intent, they should be permitted to formulate modifications and unique combinations of rules *in advance of* opportunities to play. The methods described also encourage children to modify their responses and thoughts *while they participate* in these learning experiences. Thus most of the game descriptions suggest, and sometimes require, that the learners participate actively in their own learning progress. The methods strongly recommend that the children and youth engage in pre-planning game modifications while the action is taking place, as well as in decisions about evaluation once the game has been terminated.

The ways to transfer decisions about learning to the learner has occupied the thoughts of educational philosophers since the time of Plato and Socrates. Depending upon the presence of other social-political forces and religious doctrines, educators throughout the centuries have advocated varying amounts of freedom and control within educational programs and institutions. Renaissance thinkers advocated nurturing the "natural unfolding" of the child within school programs, while their predecessors of the middle ages considered it necessary to work within strictly uniform dimensions. One of the more lucid contemporary writers to consider the manner in which decisions and freedoms should be apportioned in school has been Muska Mosston. In his books written in the late 1960s as well as in those written more recently (Mosston 1982), he has advocated that an entire "spectrum of teaching styles" be considered by teachers. Points within this spectrum have included methods that range from a strict "command" orientation, in which the teacher makes all of the decisions, to more liberal postures, which include numerous decisions formulated by the learner.[1]

Mosston postulates that it is most helpful to release decisionmaking responsibility to learners, if it is to be released at all, at times relative to the time teacher and student are together "impacting" one another. Thus, students' first decisions should be modifications of tasks occurring during the time of teacher-student impact (when they are together). The next decisions to be transferred should be evaluation decisions, generally occurring after "impact." Final decisions, which may be shifted to learners when they are intellectually ready to receive them, should be planning decisions, or those which usually involve program and task decisions prior to the time student and teacher come together.

Other thinkers about these same methodological problems and strategies have also formulated lists of what are often termed intellectual processes, thought qualities that should be considered when formulating lessons in schools (Gagne 1965; Guilford 1959; Spearman and Jones 1951). Some have suggested classification systems or taxonomies that point to the possibility that some of these qualities are somehow more important, or "harder" to acquire, than others (Bloom 1956). Memory, for example, is often relegated to a subordinate position, as contrasted to problem-solving strategies of various kinds. And, although the intellectual qualities named in these lists differ in various respects, they often include the aforementioned processes of *divergent production* (formulating a spectrum of possibilities, a form of creative thinking used often in the graphic and performing arts); *convergent thinking* (uncovering a single best solution, an ability often required in the "hard sciences"); *evaluative qualities*, which require classification, contrasting, and comparing; as well as *analysis and synthesis*, processes previously described.

---

[1]The readers not familiar with his work should consult references in the bibliography.

Rather than placing some of these functions in subordinate roles, I prefer to call some of them *support functions*, and others, especially those involved in the solution of problems of various kinds, *basic processes*. Memory and evaluative processes (including classification, contrasting, and comparing), seem to support analysis, synthesis, and divergent and convergent production, as is shown in the following chart.

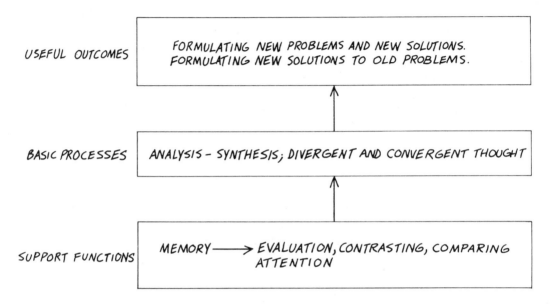

This chart suggests that memory, evaluation, and its "close relatives" contrasting and comparing, form vital and necessary supports for so-called higher level processes that impinge upon problems requiring new and creative solutions. Further, as described in Chapter 2, it could be argued that attentional qualities form an even more vital base for the acquisition of "data" through memory. It seems that little information may be acquired and retained unless reasonably high levels of attention are present for sufficient periods of time; furthermore, without data that may be retained and later recalled, complex analysis and manipulation of that information are not likely to take place.

CREATIVE TEACHING USING ACTIVE GAMES

Creativity may be defined as the bringing together of qualities, ideas, or concepts that have not been brought together before. In an attempt to help teachers use the games in this book in creative ways, I have constructed a teaching model that suggests times at which shifting of decisionmaking responsibility to learners is particularly likely to stimulate intellectual processes. Teachers may, if appropriate, attempt to fit some of these games (as well as other aspects of academic teaching) into some of the intersecting squares in this model. That is, the teacher may manage the teaching environment and formulate directions that (a) permit the learner varying amounts of freedom and (b) at the same time encourage the exercise of some of the intellectual qualities which have been discussed.

This chart and the model of flexibility it recommends may be used by the teacher in several ways. In many of the games and activities presented in the previous chapters, the descriptions and modifications sections that accompany them contain suggestions that relate to the horizontal dimension of the chart-model that follows. That is, the teacher may choose to give the participating children an increasing number of decisions and choices as the activity progresses within a single day, or as successive exposure to the tasks is experienced over a number of days. Using as an example a game involving letter identification that requires children to jump into squares containing letters, on successive exposures the children might first simply jump in the squares called by the teacher. Next an impact decision is made (coming during the time the teacher and child are actually in the lesson), by letting the children decide what square they will next jump in, and then by asking them to call the letter it contains. "Post-impact," or evaluative decisions, may next be extended to the children, as they are paired, and an "evaluation partner" is asked to score whether or not a "performing partner" is indeed jumping into the correct square as a letter is called. Finally, pre-impact decisions may be extended to the children. These involve pre-planning. In this example the students may be asked to formulate a variation of the letter-jumping game prior to playing it.

Many of the games and activities described in the beginning chapters lend themselves to movement down the following chart by the teacher. That is, the instructor may become able to explore various kinds of intellectual processes, from memory to problem solving, using some of the game-activity outlines contained in the first sections of the book. Exploration of various kinds of processes are particularly encouraged by the games in Chapter 8. But with careful "meta-cognition" on the part of the teacher (or thought about thought),[2] most of the book's activities may be enhanced.

The inclusion of various kinds of intellectual operations is easily possible within a "simple" coding game, one that requires children to react correctly by using specific movement responses that are paired with specific figures, letters, or numbers placed on a blackboard. The object is to learn that a 2 means *Jump*, to give one example. It is obvious that simple memory may be required in this game, with the memory span gradually being taxed either in length (more symbol-movement combinations to be learned), or in time (short-term or long-term memory may be "tapped" as the children are either asked to delay a response to

[2]A case could be made for the processes engaged in by the teacher when trying to encourage "meta-cognition" by students as consisting of "meta-meta-cognition"; while of course my efforts in writing this book might even be looked upon as meta-meta-meta . . . or something!

a written symbol for a minute or less, or they are asked to give correct "movement answers" to movement-symbol combinations learned the day or the week before. By using coding games, virtually all cognitive operations may be exercised, for example: (a) Divergent production may be exercised, if children are asked to formulate new movement codes and to think up new symbols, either in written form or in some other form (for instance, noises or spoken words); (b) Analysis and synthesis is required if a child is first given simple parts of a complex figure with each part standing for a simple movement, and then is given the total figure, made up of the parts, and asked to execute the more complicated movement it supposedly stands for. The child must first analyze the now more complex written figure for meaning, and then synthesize a movement composed of the parts previously learned to parts of the figure. (c) Evaluation decisions abound within this kind of "coding game" as children are asked to assess their own accuracy, the accuracy of others, the value of the activity itself, and how it might be translated into useful academic demands and operations. Thus in these and numerous other ways the creative teacher may explore various cognitive operations within the game forms presented.

Even more challenging uses of the chart may be explored. For example, the teacher may attempt to "move" conceptually both down and across the chart in an oblique direction. That is, the instructor within a given activity may carefully try to both release more and more useful decisions to the learners while at the same time provide ways in which these decisions will require different and interesting cognitive operations. Thus, to again use the example of coding games, the teacher might attempt to both transfer pre-planning decisions to the children, and at the same time suggest how they might change the game to involve divergent production, after explaining to them the meaning of that phrase.

Perhaps the ultimate use of the chart might be to present it, in parts or as a whole, to the more able students. The students might then try to discern ways in which activities found in play, as well as those used in formal physical education programs and academic tasks and operations, correspond to various "blocks" within the grid of possibilities presented on the chart. The chart might also be used as a guide for in-service education of teachers, both within academic subjects as well as with those dealing in physical-emotional development. Curricula designed during the elementary and secondary years to bring student-participants along one or both dimensions (horizontal decisionmaking and vertical cognitive-operations) might also result in student growth along lines deemed useful by both movement educators and those focusing upon classroom operations.

More and more research has begun to focus upon the outcomes of innovative curriculum formulations, not only the dimensions we have described and depicted on the chart, but others. More and more careful analyses are being made about the quantity as well as the quality of student involvement both in physical activity and in decisionmaking (Godbout, Brunelle, and Tousignant

"Decisions About Decisions"	Style I "Command Style": Teacher Makes All Decisions	Style II Shifts of Decisions *During* Teacher-Learner *Impact*	Style ... Deci... Shif... Im... E...
Memory	#1 Remember this skill.	#7 Can you remember other movements similar to this one?	
Evaluation; Classification	#2 L's T's and E's all have right angles—draw them.	#8 Mary, wat... George, he is c...	...keup ...help us ...te skill.
Analysis	#3 Tell me all the sounds in the word *bird*.	#9 If C... Ju... m...	...l ...'s plan a ...ame to help us find sounds in words.
Synthesis	#4 Now perform a... the movemen... together in c... skill.		#22 Let's make up a movement game to help us combine things.
Divergent Production	#5 Now... jum... in...	...uld June have ...ne the ...movement in three different directions?	#23 How can we encourage Mary to create her own dance?
Convergent Production		#18 Did John correctly spell the letters in the words by jumping in the squares?	#24 How can we teach letter sounds using a movement game?

1983). However, there are times when the strict teacher-directed approach seems an equal or superior method for attaining the rather narrow (in our opinion) goal of simple skill acquisition (Goldberger, Gerney, and Chamberlain 1982; Martinek, Zaichkowsky, and Cheffers 1977). On the whole, contemporary research findings indicate that student decisionmaking and intellectual involvement in curricula with "movement content" enhances a variety of qualities in children, more so than do teacher-directed programs. Among the positive outcomes enjoyed by children who have some voice in their own physical and/or movement education are improvement in attitude about activity, enhancement of their self-concept, sport skills, social helping skills, and creativity (Godbout, Brunelle, and Tousignant 1983; Goldberger, Gerney, and Chamberlain 1982; Martinek, Zaichkowsky, and Cheffers 1977; Toole and Arink 1982; Schempp, Cheffers, and Zaichkowsky 1983; Mancini, Cheffers, and Zaichkowsky 1976).

By referring to the chart, a teacher may be aided in becoming more flexible, expanding the range of behaviors likely to trigger selected intellectual qualities. A "movement educator" whose instructions traditionally suggest that a child "jumps into the hoop as many ways as possible" triggers divergent production, but if he is using a command style, he limits the range of responses that the child may make.

Teachers, upon inspection of this chart, might try to formulate games and modify their behaviors to include verbal instructions that will correspond to many, if not most, of the intersecting squares. Not all of the intersecting squares will make sense relative to an individual teacher's overall objectives. The following explanations may help the teacher, not only to aid the child to think in more flexible ways, but also to bring the learner to a point at which she may be given more decisionmaking responsibility about her own educational program.

STYLE I: *COMMAND:* ALL DECISIONS MADE BY TEACHER

In a "command mode" the effective teacher tries to transmit materials to functioning within the culture (for instance, the letters of the alphabet, what numbers mean, and the like). Materials of increasing complexity use the entire scale.

Memory.   (Square #1) Exact correspondences between inarguable combinations—for example, letters having only sound in English, or perhaps that 1 truly means one thing—are examples of effective concepts and operations within the command-memory intersect.

Evaluation/Classification.   (Square #2) Again, classification of important items within traditional classification systems may be triggered within this command mode, (for instance discriminations between upper and lower case letters, shapes, and the like). The teacher should realize that "things" are classified with increased precision as children grow older (that is, all animals are "dogs" for children of two or three years, while later dogs and cats are separate categories, and finally the child discovers that a "dog" may be placed into several categories, for instance, the dog that barks, a schnauzer, and my dog).

Analysis. (Square #3) Commands for analysis, again, should follow irrefutable dimensions, as in word attack skills and the like. When the component sounds of words are sought, this constitutes analysis.

Synthesis. (Square #4) A child's first introduction to the process of synthesis may come in the "command mode," with later more flexible teaching of this concept and exercising of this capacity appearing in the "decisionmaking" styles that follow.

Divergent Production. (Square #5) To some, the presence of divergent production opportunities within a command mode involves irreconcilable contrasts. However, if the teacher seems to "demand" divergency in tasks that are mundane and even oppressive to the learner, it may be argued that "divergency" is being demanded—"Now show me another way to jump over the line!"

Convergent Production. (Square #6) The teacher who insists upon a prolonged search for a correct or best solution is using the command style in order to elicit convergent production. At times convergency in simple pairings (for example, letters-sounds) also involves memory. However, when the tasks are complex and the search is long, more than memory is elicited.

STYLE II: *TASK PHASE:* DECISIONS DURING IMPACT SHIFTED TO LEARNER

Shifts of Decisions During Impact. The shifts of decisions during impact can afford the teacher the most comfortable kinds of ways to begin to involve the learner. During impact, decisions may be made gradually—at first, only a few of the many possible decisions may be transferred to the learner, and then if successful, more may be placed in the learner's hands.

Memory. (Square #7) Recall memory may often be elicited with requests made for "remembering" during impact periods. Relationships and categorization abilities may be triggered (for example, a child may be asked to remember what other words start with the same sound, or what other movements are similar to or different from (or opposite) the movements being performed).

Evaluation/Classification. (Square #8) Some might question whether evaluation decisions may be truly carried out during impact, but I believe they can be. That is, as a child is in action, she may be asked to engage in evaluative self-talk, while others may also be asked to provide evaluative feedback to the child while the action is in progress. Thus evaluation, during this phase and in Style III, can consist of evaluation from peers, from teachers, or from the child herself in the form of "self correction and evaluation."

Analysis. (Square #9) Opportunities abound for the exercise of analytic competencies in a movement context. A complex movement may be demonstrated, for example, while children try to find single words that may best describe the movement to another child who has not seen the original. The nonobserver's powers of synthesis are later taxed, if when brought into the room, he must try to demonstrate the complex movement, given only "key" description words.

Synthesis. (Square #10) Synthesis may be engaged in during the "impact period" as components are combined by the learners when asked by the teacher to do so. Formulation of gymnastic and dance routines represent opportunities for "impact" synthesis.

Divergent Production. (Square #11) Divergent production during impact is what is most commonly seen and elicited in movement education programs, as children are asked to display flexibility of responses. It should be remembered, however, that divergency and convergency represent extremes on a scale, and that tasks generally range themselves on this scale depending upon the directions given and the nature of the task.

Convergent Production. (Square #12) Convergent, or best-solution, tasks are sometimes harder to formulate in a movement context than are those that exercise divergent production. However, instructions that limit "the correctness" of a response, or problems that may only be satisfied with a single type of movement or a single movement represent this type of task within an "impact situation."

STYLE III: *EVALUATION DECISIONS:*
POST-IMPACT DECISIONS SHIFTED TO LEARNER

Intellectual processes occurring in this style involve looking back in time, the recalling of the quality of processes engaged in by other children or by the learner himself. For the most part, the learning opportunities in this Style involve evaluation (evaluation of self or of others). At times, however, evaluation in this Style requires that the child really understands the processes he has just viewed or experienced. Within both Styles III and IV, the participating children must be able to engage in a considerable amount of thinking about thinking, or "meta-cognitive" behaviors. Thus the teacher must go one step further than the children. She must engage in meta-meta-cognitive behaviors! She must think about how to aid people to think about thinking.

Memory. (Square #13) In this type of task the child must evaluate the quality of the memory displayed in a previous exercise. The evaluation may be of the quality of the memory task and/or of the memory and perhaps the retention displayed by the learner himself or by other children.

Evaluation/Classification. (Square #14) Again the child must evaluate—in this case the quality of evaluation itself! The child may be asked to determine if the previous learner might have formed more classes of objects or of movements, as well as to evaluate the accuracy of the classification and evaluation that had taken place in the past exercise.

Synthesis. (Square #16) The post-impact evaluator may be able to discover both the quality of the synthesis that has just occurred, as well as to determine how the components might have been combined into other wholes, such as, "How might you have combined the movements in this routine? What are the advantages of your way of combining them vs. the ways that have been used by the previous learner?"

Analysis. (Square #15) The child must really understand (a) what analysis is, and (b) the quality of the analytic functions that have just occurred. There may be more than one way to analyze what has just occurred, which may be discovered during this post-impact phase.

Divergent Production. (Square #17) Often during this post-impact evaluation of divergent production, the evaluator can suggest additional components that have been overlooked by a previous learner engaged in divergent production. "What other ways might you use to get the ball in the basket?"

Convergent Production. (Square #18) Post-impact evaluation of the qualities of convergent production assesses whether a single best solution arrived at is truly the best! The evaluator may find an equally good, or better solution to a problem she has just observed being "solved." "Are you certain that that is the only way that movement task, involving those directions, may be performed?"

STYLE IV: *PRE-IMPACT PLANNING:*
PROGRAMMING DECISIONS SHIFTED TO LEARNER

This final style "model" requires the most sophisticated intellectual problem-solving behavior. The learner must thoroughly understand each process and at the same time understand how one may operationalize each process in terms of a game. It will often be found that not all children can understand and formulate activities that will "tap into" all the intellectual processes listed. Thus, for example some children may become able to make up memory games, but remain unable to understand the processes of convergent production, and therefore unable to make up activities that stimulate those processes.

Memory. (Square #19) Discussions of various dimensions of memory (that is, auditory, visual, verbal, short-term, long-term, medium-term, and recall vs. recognition memory) might elicit new memory games after a child or group has been exposed to one type of activity. The usefulness of forgetting (that is, selective retention) might also be worked into games.

Evaluation. (Square #20) Subprocesses of evaluation, including contrasting (how are two things different or the same) and comparing, may be worked into this pre-planning teaching style, with regard to classification. A simple classification game may be expanded to include other classification items and systems (for instance, after classifying movements, how many objects and ideas be classified? etc.).

Analysis. (Square #21) Changing from a movement context to an academic context may be attempted during the pre-planning phase of games involving analysis. Moreover, the new games invented during this pre-planning phase might be designed to elicit new levels of analytic sophistication that were previously demonstrated by the children's peers.

Synthesis. (Square #22) Children may be asked to formulate new games involving synthesis of previous movements (for example, group them into both larger and smaller categories during a pre-planning break, within this style). As is true within this entire style, failure to understand what synthesis truly consists of will doom efforts to formulate lessons in this subtle process. Putting together the parts of a dance routine represents synthesis.

Divergent Production. (Square #23) In this pre-planning exercise children may be asked to apply their understanding of what divergent production is all about in a movement context, to other creative endeavors including making up a dance, drawing a picture, writing a play, and the like. Experiments with new games may also attempt to deal with games and instructions that elicit varying degrees of convergent and divergent production, with discussions of how this continuum concept is found in other aspects of life underlying the formulation of such games.

   Convergent Production.   (Square #24) Children dealing with the formulation of games and programs eliciting convergent production might compare such activities to simple memory and try to ascertain the difference (that is, memory is commanded, and convergent production is an evolution, a process of discovery).

   The tasks suggested by this model represent experiences, both operational and intellectual, that both learners and teachers may confront. The tasks present new ways in which the teacher may free the learner both to think and at the same time to think in increasingly sophisticated and intricate ways about problems of various complexity. The use of this model with children of various ages and within both academic and "movement" contexts is a difficult, but at the same time, a fascinating undertaking, which may be extremely rewarding to both teacher and learner.

A WORD ABOUT SELF-TALK

   In many of the games, particularly those aiming to elicit better self-control, a procedure called "self-talk" was employed. This procedure may be employed as well in a variety of ways through the book, and when using the model of "styles and processes" just outlined. This technique represents an important, well-researched addition to teachers' "armaments" for use in the "firing lines" of their classrooms. The procedure has limitations and requires patience and understanding; not only of the technique itself, but also of the client-children to whom it is applied. Children with poor language and speech skills may find its use blunted. However, even with these children the teacher may aid in the organization of thought, the focusing of attention, and in the careful planning of both motor tasks and those found in the classroom (Meichenbaum and Asnarow 1979).

   These tools, when applied, should be carefully sequenced and modified to fit the developmental level of the child. Sequences include shortening sentences, as the act is acquired; moving from sentences to sentence fragments and then to single words. Likewise, the speech may be moved from outside to inside the child. That is, the child may be asked to exhibit vocalizations that all can hear at first, when they plan and correct themselves in tasks. Later the child may be encouraged to whisper self-directions, and still later to voice commands and corrections internally.

   The whole point of this kind of exercise in self-direction is to change how the child thinks about task execution and about thinking itself. Theorists and researchers describing the process allude to a "cognitive click" that often occurs somewhere inside the head (beyond the reach of hard-minded neurologists!), which signals the true acceptance of a thought that had appeared earlier only in a superficial, voiced form.

SUMMARY AND OVERVIEW

The material in this final chapter deals with several important themes found in the activities described in the text. One of the themes dealt with involves provisions for transferring operations, concepts, and processes found in active games to classroom activities and operations. Ways of eliciting transfer include doing a lot of transferable things and building cognitive bridges between two tasks, or types of tasks, between which it is desired that transfer take place.

The major emphasis in this final section revolves around a teaching model. The model has two primary dimensions. One of these describes how decisions may be shifted to the learner in an orderly manner. It is hoped that with more learner involvement more acquisition of skills and concepts will take place. The second major dimension of the model includes reference to commonly cited intellectual operations. The ones discussed include several "support" processes (including memory, categorization, and evaluation) as well as several more primary and complex mental processes (divergent and convergent production, analysis, and synthesis). The model, furthermore, presents ways in which these dimensions interact. Examples of ways in which one might not only shift decisions about learning to the learner, but at the same time trigger increasingly sophisticated intellectual processes are also shown.

The chapter concludes with a discussion of "self-talk," an important operation treated within several parts of the text. Through the use of self-talk, children may not only become more effective thinkers but should begin to acquire the ability to think about thinking—to exhibit "meta-cognitive" behavior.

Overall, this chapter and the ones that precede it, try to encourage teachers not only to help children become able to think about thinking but to think about how children think about thinking themselves!

Finally, it was hoped that the games presented will make a happy and significant addition to children's total learning programs. Because of the vigor they involve, the high levels of attention they require, and the high visibility of their outcomes, these methods have posted good records of success in schools throughout the world.

BIBLIOGRAPHY

BLOOM, B.S.   (Ed.). *Taxonomy of educational objectives. Handbook I: Cognitive domain.* New York: D. McKay, 1956.

BRUNER, J.S.   The course of cognitive growth. *American Psychologist*, 1964, *19*, 1-15.

GAGNE, R.W.   *The conditions of learning.* New York: Holt, Rinehart & Winston, 1965.

GODBOUT, P., BRUNELLE, J., and TOUSIGNANT, M.   Academic learning time in elementary and secondary physical education classes. *Research Quarterly for Exercise and Sport*, 1983, *54*, 11-19.

GOLDBERGER, M., GERNEY, P., and CHAMBERLAIN, J.   The effects of three styles of teaching on the psychomotor performance and social skill development of fifth grade children. *Research Quarterly for Exercise and Sport*, 1982, *53*, 116-124.

GUILFORD, J.P.   *Intelligence, creativity and their educational implications.* San Diego: Knapp, 1968.

MANCINI, V., CHEFFERS, J., and ZAICHKOWSKY, L.   Decisionmaking in elementary school children: Effects on attitudes and interactions. *Research Quarterly*, 1976, *47*, 349-357.

MARTINEK, T.J., ZAICHKOWSKY, L.D., and CHEFFERS, J.T.F.   Decisionmaking in elementary age children: Effects on motor skills and self-concept. *Research Quarterly for Exercise and Sport*, 1977, *48*, 349-357.

MEICHENBAUM, D., and ASNAROW, J.R.   Cognitive-behavior modification and metacognitive development: Implications for the classroom. In P. Kendall and S. Hollon (Eds.), *Cognitive-behavioral interventions: Theory, research and procedures.* New York: Academic Press, 1979.

MOSSTON, M.   *Teaching physical education.* (2nd ed.) Belmont, CA: Wadsworth, 1982.

PIAGET, J.   *The child's conception of the world.* Totowa, NJ: Littlefield, Adams, 1965.

SCHEMPP, P.G., CHEFFERS, J.T.F., and ZAICHKOWSKY, L.D.   Influence of decisionmaking on attitudes, creativity, motor skills, and self-concept in elementary children. *Research Quarterly for Exercise and Sport*, 1983, *54*, 183-189.

SPEARMAN, C., and JONES, L.W.   *Human ability.* London: MacMillan, 1951.

TOOLE, T., and ARINK, E.A.   Movement education: Its effect on motor skill performance. *Research Quarterly for Exercise and Sport*, 1982, *53*, 156-162.

DATE DUE

DEMCO 38-297